LIBERALIZATION AGAINST
DEMOCRACY

INDIANA SERIES IN MIDDLE EAST STUDIES

MARK TESSLER

GENERAL EDITOR

LIBERALIZATION AGAINST DEMOCRACY

THE LOCAL POLITICS
OF ECONOMIC REFORM
IN TUNISIA

STEPHEN J. KING

INDIANA
University Press
Bloomington & Indianapolis

This book is a publication of

Indiana University Press
601 North Morton Street
Bloomington, IN 47404-3797 USA

http://iupress.indiana.edu

Telephone orders 800-842-6796
Fax orders 812-855-7931
Orders by e-mail iuporder@indiana.edu

The paper used in this publication meets the minimum requirements of American National Standard for Information Sciences—Permanence of Paper for Printed Library Materials, ANSI Z39.48-1984.

Manufactured in the United States of America

Library of Congress Cataloging-in-Publication Data

King, Stephen J. (Stephen Juan), date
Liberalization against democracy : the local politics of economic reform in Tunisia / Stephen J. King.
p. cm. — (Indiana series in Middle East studies)
Includes bibliographical references and index.
ISBN 0-253-34212-0 (alk. paper) — ISBN 0-253-21583-8 (pbk. : alk. paper)
1. Democracy—Tunisia. 2. Local government—Tunisia. 3. Structural adjustment (Economic policy)—Tunisia. I. Title. II. Series.
JQ3336 .K56 2003
320.9611—dc21

2002014600

1 2 3 4 5   08 07 06 05 04 03

❖ TO THE BELOW ZEROS OF TEBOURBA ❖
AND TO JOAN YENGO.
A SPECIAL THANKS TO FRANKIE KING,
WHO KEPT WALKING UP THE
HILL TO SCHOOL.

CONTENTS

Illustrations follow page 109

TABLES

PREFACE

THE OPPORTUNITY TO participate in and observe a rural community in the midst of widespread land privatization and other elements of a standard structural adjustment program spurred the early research that gave rise to this book. Two years spent in the patronage-ridden Moroccan countryside had led me to question whether conventional economic reforms would necessarily lead to the creation of the self-help market-oriented society and more democratic politics presumably envisioned by the World Bank and Tunisian architects of Tunisia's neo-liberal economic transformation.

I arrived in rural northwest Tunisia in 1993 and settled in the village of Tebourba for a twelve-month stay. Initially, I attempted to take a snapshot of Tebourba's political community. I began with participant observation and qualitative interviews of approximately forty-five minutes in order to determine who controlled what resources. At this point, I worked backward to discover how people arrived at their relative power positions. A portion of the interviews explored the strategies people used to obtain these resources. I also explored village institutions of welfare and insurance for the poor and the role of formal politics, including local and national elections and the farmers' union. I interviewed officials and members of all social categories involved in agriculture. Most of the interviews took place in the fields of the farms themselves and in the offices of local officials. A Tunisian colleague and friend helped me arrange and conduct the early interviews and aided me with the transition from the Moroccan to the Tunisian dialect of Arabic. I conducted the later interviews alone. This textured portrait of contemporary political community in Tebourba as it undertakes market-oriented changes can be found in chapter 4 of this book. The names of the people of the community have been changed to protect their anonymity. The translations from Arabic and French are my own.

In order to more fully understand political community in the past in the region and the impact of structural adjustment on political community, I conducted archival and library research, consulting in particular the very useful earlier study of Tebourba by Mira Zussman. The historical perspective of my work can be found in chapter 3. Together, chapters 3 and 4 detail how state elites deliberately stimulated cultural traditionalism in order to sustain neo-liberal reforms; economic reform at the local level strengthened traditional patronage and decreased formal political participation.

In my case the local view of neo-liberal economic transformation led to broader questions about the connection between economic reform and political change at the national level. Chapter 1 of this book explores the theoretical underpinnings of the generally accepted proposition that economic liberalization leads to political liberalization. Chapter 2, however, argues to the contrary that economic reform in Tunisia as a whole subverted democratic tendencies.

A Social Science Research Council international pre-dissertation grant and a smaller grant from the Woodrow Wilson Center for International Affairs at Princeton University supported a six-week visit to Tunisia in early 1993. During that trip, the Tunisian scholar El-Baki Hermassi suggested Tebourba as a research site and planted the idea of a study that would piggy-back on Mira Zussman's earlier community study. The long period of field work conducted in 1993–94 was generously funded by a Fulbright grant. A post-doctoral fellowship from the Ford Foundation provided me with a year's funding to revise this book at the Carnegie Endowment for International Peace. I am especially grateful to the fine library staff at that institution. Julia Voelker from Georgetown University was a particularly able research assistant during the editing process. I would also like to personally thank Atul Kohli, Lisa Anderson, John Bailey, and especially John Waterbury for their bracing intellectual engagement with my work.

LIBERALIZATION AGAINST DEMOCRACY

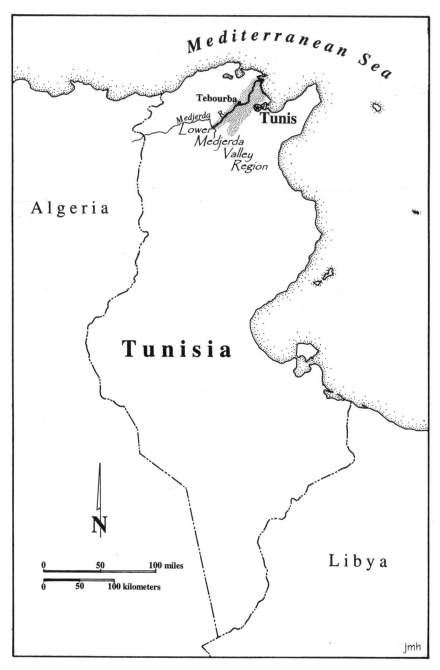

Tunisian "socialism" began with an agricultural cooperative movement in the Lower Medjerda Valley region of Tunisia. Tebourba, the primary field site of this study, is located in the heart of this region.

$$\cdot \quad 1 \quad \cdot$$

LIBERALIZATION AGAINST DEMOCRACY

> The sharing of resources within communal organizations and reliance on
> ties with powerful patrons were recurrent ways peasants strove to reduce
> risks and to improve their stability, and both were condoned and fre-
> quently supported by the state.
> —Eric Wolf, *Peasant Wars of the Twentieth Century*

IN THE MID-1990s, Tebourba, a large village in the fertile northwest region of
Tunisia, began implementing land policies that were part of a structural adjustment program (SAP). The privatization of land was the final stage in the
dismantling of the country's socialist project, as the state attempted to complete market-oriented changes that it had begun cautiously in the early 1970s.
State-managed agricultural production cooperatives had formed the core of
Tunisian socialism, and Tebourba is located in the heart of a region dominated
by these cooperatives. The privatization of state farms under Tunisia's SAP involved a major shift in asset distribution, which caused considerable social and
political turmoil. Large landholders were the primary beneficiaries of this land
reform.

The impact of these trends in Tebourba was reflected in the attitudes expressed to me by local inhabitants while I was doing field work there in the
1990s; they are summed up in the following remarks made to me by three
people in very different socioeconomic positions:

A poor peasant: "The workers have become beggars. The sun shines on
everyone. Normally the state looks after us all. Why give the land to the rich?
They already have land. If you give them more they will no longer think of
the poor. What are they going to do with more, buy another car? It's no good.
You find people with a thousand hectares while others won't even have one
hectare. The poor wanted land. Some farmers before got land and they're doing well. [In the early 1970s, a small amount of state land was distributed to
former cooperative workers.] If you have connections you can get land. Those
who were fired like me always go to the administration asking for work. We

tell them, "You fired us, so give me something to buy bread." Nothing happens. The cooperative used to employ eighty people, but now only thirty work there. Those thirty are almost always women because they are paid less. They work for twelve hours a day with someone standing over them the whole time. Men require four dinars a day [at the time of this interview, one dinar equaled approximately one U.S. dollar] while the women work for three-something. You know the ministry tells them to pay us five dinars a day.

"The poor will always stay poor around here. The poor lack rain and grass for their animals. The rich won't allow them to graze on their land. Before you could graze your animals and they would also give you money. Now the rich don't give you anything. I went to a rich farmer and asked for a little wheat. He said, "Get out, God will help you." Another man, rich with a 404 truck, asked and he gave him the wheat. The rich and the administrators help each other. For example, the Hajj will give ten or twenty kilos of wheat to the poor, but he'll give a lot more to the rich without them coming by. ["Hajj" means a person who has made the pilgrimage to Mecca; here the speaker is referring to the largest local landowner.]

"If there's assistance from the state the ʿumda will give out 50 percent of it and give the rest to his friends or keep it. [An ʿumda (plural ʿumad) is a community or neighborhood leader. Formerly, the ʿumda would be a *shaykh,* or tribal leader. Currently, state agents fill these positions with party loyalists, not all of whom are *shuykh.*] If you complain the ʿumda will create worse problems. To get assistance you go to the *délégué* [the local representative of the regional governor]. Before the délégué will help you, he asks the ʿumda. My four-year-old son needed medicine for heart disease, but the ʿumda said I didn't need anything. That I'm doing fine. If you go into my house you'll know how poor I am. I went to the délégué when my son got sicker; he made the ʿumda deliver the money for medicine to my door."

An ʿumda: "The poor are reluctant to ask for aid. The ʿumda meets with party members who try to figure out who needs help and what to present. Several sector heads will meet with their ʿumda and during alʿEid al-Kabir, alʿEid as-Saghir, Ramadan, and other holidays they distribute the aid. We get the assistance from the wealthy, who are friends of the party. Some of the rich give directly to the poor. On religious holidays some people will give around thirteen dinars to a poor family, or a sack of wheat. Since I've been here we've had good community solidarity. There was some trouble a year or so ago and they talked about building a National Guard office across the street. However, after I worked together with the rich to help out the poor, things quieted down. Just this year there were eighty gift packages given out during Ramadan in my sector."

A rich farmer: "Large farmers give potatoes in every harvest; first to relatives and neighbors and then to the poor. The ʿumda gathers the potatoes from the rich and hands them out. Each family receives a hundred kilos of potatoes, and then sells some of them. Clothes and money can be given through the ʿumda or directly on holidays. However, most of these people don't deserve it. The poor come to us for the *zakat* or aid, but they don't come to work. We can't find people to work with olives because the work is too hard. They want comfort or they want assistance without work. If they come to the house we help the elderly but not the young.

"In general there is moral decay here. We have thefts and even murder. Many people cause problems in the street. Even the rich are getting spoiled. They are not doing their job of presenting new projects to society."

Presumably, state-led economic liberalization in Tunisia was designed to create a self-help market-oriented society and conditions that would facilitate a transition to democratic rule. However, this book argues that neo-liberal economic transformation led to the retraditionalization of local politics and the resurgence of clientelism. For most peasants the new market arrangements have increased risk but not opportunity. A moral economy at the local level is being revived during state-led economic liberalization. The bureaucratic establishment and rural notables have promoted the revival of neo-traditional political and economic behavior emphasizing reciprocal moral obligations, Islamic values, and redistributive institutions, in order to head off equity concerns raised by economic reform.

During this same period the small peasantry in Tebourba withdrew from participation in the national agricultural union and other collective organizations in which they had been active in the 1970s (Zussman 1992). However, although state policy had turned decidedly against them during the decade, peasants continued to support Tunisia's hegemonic state party in municipal and national elections; the state party received more than 98 percent of the overall vote in the municipal and legislative elections of 1994 and 1999. Poor peasants claimed that only the state party could possibly deliver any benefits (King 1997). Rural notables were also in a better position to deliver the votes of their peasant clienteles to their bureaucratic allies. Overall, during economic liberalization, agricultural laborers and the small peasantry withdrew from real participation in formal political institutions.

In the Tunisian case, the local context provides a window to changes in the national political economy. The reemergence of traditional politics in rural areas has helped to reconfigure authoritarianism in the country as a whole. Accelerated economic liberalization in Tunisia has coincided with coalition politics that changed a populist authoritarian regime to one characterized by

economic projects designed to bolster large landowners and the urban bourgeoisie.

Tunisian policymakers pursued gradual economic liberalization from 1970
until 1986, when market reforms were accelerated under the auspices of IMF
stabilization and World Bank structural adjustment programs. Gradual economic liberalization in Tunisia in the 1970s and 1980s posed tremendous challenges to Tunisia's populist authoritarian regime. A rising working class cham-
pioned democracy and applied pressure on the single-party system, leading
some elites and other social groups to become advocates of democratic reform.
During Tunisia's first wave of economic opening, *infitah* (1970–86), market-
oriented policies initially produced a positive aggregate economic growth pic-
ture, but by the end of the 1970s growth in GDP had dropped by half and unemployment had doubled (Anderson 1986, 242). The new hardships spurred
workers and students to stage frequent demonstrations and strikes. In 1978, the
Tunisian national labor union (Union Générale Tunisienne de Travail, UGTT)
organized the country's first general strike. By that time, complaints about economic grievances had grown to include calls for democratic reform and other
explicitly political demands (Alexander 1996, 183). The general strike threatened the viability of the state as the police and army clashed with workers and
students. Islamist groups, fearing the rise of the left, became more politicized
and critical of the regime as well (Hamdi 1998, 32).

The challenges from below led Tunisian authorities to experiment with
political democratization (Anderson 1986, 246). Multiparty elections were
held for the first time in 1981. However, the democratic reforms of that year
never took hold. Elements of the hegemonic state party apparently had second
thoughts and interfered with the elections to ensure that not a single opposition candidate was elected (Anderson 1986, 248).

In 1986, Tunisia began a second round of economic reform and political
change. The regime began implementing standard IMF stabilization and World
Bank structural adjustment policies. In addition to redistributing land up the
social scale, these policies primarily targeted the wealthiest segment of the urban bourgeoisie (Payne 1991). At the same time, the political challenges of the
late 1970s, which had never been completely quelled, began to regain momentum. Habib Bourguiba, the country's only post-independence president, did
not survive these continued clashes between state and society. Bourguiba was
removed from power in 1987 in a bloodless coup, after escalating confronta-
tions with Islamists that left the country on the brink of civil war.

The intensification of market-oriented reforms and competitive democracy were the major planks of the new president, General Zein al-Abidine Ben Ali (Payne 1991; Zartman 1991, 9). The new leader came to power in 1987 with a pluralistic vision of society and politics in "the new era," giving cause for hope that elite attitudes favored democratization. After the 1989 presidential and legislative elections Tunisia was widely considered to be in the midst of a democratic transition (Zartman 1991).

However, in the past decade, Tunisian authorities have shown a growing intolerance for dissent, criticism, or opposition of any kind. Rather than giving rise to a democratizing or liberalizing trend, the period of accelerated marketization in Tunisia has been associated with the hardening of authoritarianism (despite favorable aggregate economic growth rates). The combination of economic crisis and neo-liberal reforms weakened the bargaining power of the organized labor movement, which dropped its demands for democratic reforms. Indeed, beginning in 1989, the UGTT began participating in new corporatist institutions and acquiesced to a new period of authoritarianism (Alexander 1996, 195). Tunisia's state party reconstituted authoritarianism, supported primarily by large landowners and the urban bourgeoisie, both of whom were poised to profit most from new market-oriented policies.

The Tunisian experience contradicts much of the conventional wisdom about economic and political reform in the developing world. Structural adjustment theory places most of its hopes for equity on the increasing welfare of the entire agricultural sector (Commander 1989; Nelson 1992, 227). Many theorists expected that the market reforms implemented throughout the developing world in the 1980s and 1990s would enhance the prospects of democratic rule.[1] However, market reforms made many Tunisian farmers worse off economically and older forms of clientelism reappeared, undermining the prospects for political democratization. Socioeconomic conditions (increasing inequality and a shift of power away from subordinate classes) and the habits

---

1. Diamond (1992, 1999) emphasized the end of rent-seeking, political corruption, and the diffusion of political power as economic resources became more diffuse. His work also relies on the insights of Lipset (1959), who underlined socioeconomic growth, a bourgeoisie that favors democracy, and the development of a political culture conducive to democratic governance. Waisman (1992) argued for the strong link between market-oriented economic changes and democratization. Huntington (1991) pointed to a linkage to the international economic system that promotes democracy. O'Donnell and Schmitter (1986) focused on the choices of elites for democracy at a time of economic uncertainty and changing international norms favoring democratic rule. As advocates of neo-liberal economic policies, agencies such as the World Bank, the IMF, and USAID certainly hoped that markets would foster democracy.

of single-party rule were much more important to regime outcome than the stated choices of political elites well rehearsed in the language of democratic transition.

In sum, recent market-oriented reforms in Tunisia have reinforced clientelism, corporatism, and authoritarianism, as well as bringing a heavy dose of repression. An understanding of these counterintuitive findings requires a closer look at the empirical basis and theoretical underpinnings of the postulated linkages between market reforms and political development.

The recent literature suggesting that markets foster democracy is largely based on cross-national aggregate data studies (Diamond 1992, 1999; Huntington 1991; Waisman 1992; Barro 1996). In contrast, this book explores the links between economic reform and political change from the perspective of a theoretically informed case study, with a particular focus on the local level. An in-depth field study of the economic liberalization–political liberalization hypothesis illustrates how state economic policy and ideology make themselves felt at the grass roots. Tracing the process in this way sheds light on the pathways and causal mechanisms associated with the relationship between economics and politics. The divergence of the key conclusions in this book from the conventional wisdom suggests that the method selected and the level of analysis may influence research findings. These issues deserve further investigation in future studies of the politics of economic reform.

Local-level authoritarian trends in Tunisia during state-led economic liberalization mirror those at the national level (I discuss this in chapter 2). Tunisia is situated in the semi-arid tropics, a vast zone girdling the world. Mexico, India, and much of the Middle East and Sahelian Africa lie in the same zone. Rainfed agriculture, supplemented by groundwater irrigation, predominates in this zone, as does village habitation. Land distribution is typically skewed; production typically varies enormously with rainfall. Many countries in the semi-arid tropics are undergoing structural adjustment, so the lessons learned in Tunisia may have wider applicability.

The rest of this introductory chapter reviews the theoretical literature linking economic and political change, and gives an overview of possible market-oriented policies. I argue that a shared-growth approach that specifically targets small enterprises and the small peasantry would likely have fostered democracy in the Tunisian case in a way that a conventional structural adjustment program, especially beneficial to economic elites, did not. The second chapter introduces the politics of neo-liberal economic transformation in Tunisia as a whole. The third chapter turns to the countryside, with a particular focus on the rural setting of Tebourba. The fourth chapter expands on my assertion that local politics have been retraditionalized and clientelism has resurged in this large village. The fifth chapter challenges structural adjustment theory, which locates the greatest equity gains from market economic reforms in rural areas. In the conclusion, I synthesize the argument and delineate its significance both for Tunisia and for the broader study of economic and political change in late-developing countries.

Theories of Regime Change

What are the determinants of regime outcomes? An earlier literature, dominant in the 1950s and 1960s, focused on economic modernization as the key to democratic opening. Modernization theory was developed to counter Marxist theories of political change. Thus, in this approach, industrialization and capitalist development mobilized society in a way that altered traditional political culture and social organization (Lerner 1958; Deutsch 1961; Almond and Coleman 1960); the shift in the relative power of conflicting class interests that is a central feature of economic modernization was both feared and avoided in the analysis (Rueschemeyer, Stephens, and Stephens 1992, 49).

The work of Seymour Martin Lipset (1959) addressed the issue of economic forces more directly. Using cross-national quantitative research strongly linking economic development and democracy, Lipset developed a comprehensive theoretical interpretation of these findings. He shared with modernization theory a focus on social mobilization and the centrality of political culture, but placed more emphasis on class developments. A segment of the middle classes, the bourgeoisie, with its growing economic assets, has a particularly strong interest in accountable public officials. Increased wealth also mollifies the lower classes and turns them away from revolutionary politics. Additionally, a growing economy makes the rich less hostile to democracy because they have less to fear from the poor. Lipset also suggested that economic development contributed to democracy by giving rise to civil society. Civil society was defined along the lines of de Tocqueville as a large number of voluntary intermediate organizations that collectively increase political participation, enhance political skills, generate and diffuse new opinions, and inhibit the state or other domineering forces from monopolizing political power (Diamond 1992, 117). In sum, different strands of modernization theory established cultural and socioeconomic prerequisites for democratization. While mostly uncomfortable addressing class developments, the literature assumes that the bourgeoisie support democratization.

Modernization theory has been heavily criticized. Its conceptions of political culture seemed crude and ethnocentric. While focusing on increasing political participation and mobilization, many of its theorists did not recognize that the intricacies of this process occur during industrial revolutions characterized by class conflict. There was insufficient effort to integrate domestic and international dynamics. Some challenged the view of the bourgeoisie as the dominant democratizing class agent (Rueschemeyer, Stephens, and Stephens 1992). Modernization theory did not adequately interpret the link between capitalist economic development and democratization. The theory cannot be fruitfully used to assess the potential for market-oriented reforms to promote political development. Unfortunately, the current democratization literature, when it addresses economic variables at all, tends to fall back on the assumptions of modernization theory.

Present-day theorizing on democratization de-emphasizes social structure.[2] An elite-centered, process-oriented approach has become virtually hegemonic in studies of political development (Collier 1999a, 8). For O'Donnell and Schmitter, the authors most associated with the transitions literature, the dominant characteristic of regime transition is uncertainty, which frees actors from structural constraints (O'Donnell and Schmitter 1986). For Linz and Stepan (1978), the crucial variable in transitions to democracy is political leadership in the face of social and structural strains. An essential precondition is that leaders, whatever their other goals, be committed to the establishment and survival of democratic institutions for themselves. Thus, in this approach, democracy is regarded as the product of strategic calculations by enterprising politicians, who craft democracy (Encarnacion 2000). Elite pacts to establish consensus facilitate this process.

The transitions literature is most concerned with how the democratization process begins, and this priority leads its authors to their focus on actor choices.

---

2. Dankwart Rustow (1970) pioneered this process-oriented approach. Rustow argued that stalemates between entrenched social forces led political leaders to institutionalize some crucial aspect of democratic rule. During a habituation phase, politicians and citizens committed themselves to democratic rules and procedures. This process could begin without socioeconomic or cultural prerequisites, or even leaders committed to democracy. The process-oriented approach in the tradition of Rustow became even more focused on the elite, and less on conflicts between social classes.

Regardless of the prevailing socioeconomic conditions and political culture in a country, "democracy still has to be chosen, implemented, and perpetuated by agents, real live political actors with their distinctive interests, passions, memories, and why not virtue. . . . No doubt individuals will be constrained by developmental and cultural factors, but there is still plenty of room for making right or wrong choices" (Schmitter 1992, 158–59). This theoretical orientation allows pivotal actors to be identified and institutional benchmarks established for a transition to democratic rule (Encarnacion 2000). The framework also lends itself to a concentration on the procedural and institutional aspects of democracy, such as the normalization of the electoral process.

The transitions literature's useful shift of analysis to particular actors involved in episodes of regime change and democratic benchmarks can, however, also lead to a peculiar isolation of the political dimension.[3] The separation of polity, economy, and society is radical in some of the works. Diamond, Linz, and Lipset, for example, use the term "democracy" to "signify a political system [that is] separate and apart from the economic system to which it is joined" (quoted in Cammack 1997, 221). For Diamond, historical and structural forces are somehow abstract and play no role in democratic development. Instead, democratic change is about "individuals and groups choosing, innovating, and taking risks" (Diamond 1999, xii). Apparently these choices are made in splendid isolation from the historical legacies and the relations of power that are generally important in economic, social, and political life.

In this literature, state elites choose to pursue democratic changes with limited input from societal actors. Negotiation with the opposition is emphasized, but the transition is conceptualized as beginning with splits among authoritarian incumbents. Again, the origins of these divisions are abstracted away from socioeconomic struggles (Collier 1999a, 7). Political openings are initiated by regime elites. These openings may then be exploited by various social forces, who were not the catalysts for regime change (O'Donnell and Schmitter 1986, 55).

The transitions literature analytically separates democratization into transition and consolidation phases, and defines the process of democratic consolidation in terms of elite and mass acceptance of key political institutions, in particular the electoral mechanism (Huntington 1991, 267, suggests a two-turnover test). The process is also largely dependent on elite crafting. Political

---

3. For an incisive critique of recent scholarship's tendency to separate polity and economy, see Cammack 1997.

elites are viewed as the agents who choose to institutionalize democracy and cultivate a democratic culture among the masses (Gunther, Diamandouros, and Puhle 1995; Mainwaring and Scully 1995; Diamond 1999). This emphasis leads much of the recent scholarship on democratic consolidation to focus on the (elite-led) formation of effective party systems (Schmitter 1992).

Theorizing about regime change with light regard for social structure leaves many questions unanswered. What are the origins of elite preferences? Could they be institutional? Are they influenced by social forces? What is the impact of economic change on the strategic interaction of elites? In this historical juncture, markets are ascendant, with enormous implications for the distribution of welfare and the evolution of new political arrangements. The global economy impinges heavily on domestic political dynamics. Overall, economic and political systems appear to be tightly wound together.

The transitions literature partially addresses these issues by emphasizing the elite crafting of democracy while also advocating market-oriented reforms. Diamond (1992, 482) contends that statist policies entrench corruption as a means of advancement, and tend to intensify political struggles by concentrating economic decisions in the hands of the state. Waisman (1992) asserts that statist policies stunt economic growth and the bourgeoisie, a class poised to press for democratic change. Huntington (1991) favors recent market-oriented policies because they lead to economic development, which facilitates democratization and links countries to an international system disposed toward democratic rule. For O'Donnell and Schmitter (1986, 45–47), a neo-corporatist mode of policymaking can evolve to facilitate a simultaneous market and democratic transition. Most of these analysts, in passing, acknowledge the dire impact of increasing economic inequality on democracy, but all fail to interrogate the distributional implications of current market-reform policies. Indeed, with their emphasis on changes in political culture (generally abstracted from class conflicts and economic conditions) and the democratizing potential of a more powerful bourgeoisie, they appear to assume that recent economic reforms will promote economic development and democracy in the manner suggested by modernization theory.

Although the transitions literature takes a position on market-oriented reforms, its actor-based analytic framework, inclined to eschew economic variables, does not fully explore the links between economic and political change, or between social structure and actor choice. Some of the questions involved become accessible through historically grounded political economy approaches. Instead of seeing democratization as the outcome of elite bargaining, these works emphasize the importance of relative class balance and class pressures from below.

Barrington Moore's (1966) class account demonstrated that the landed upper classes have historically been democracy's greatest opponents. In essence, Moore showed in the case of England how capitalism weakened this class while strengthening the bourgeoisie, a strong democratizing force. Rueschemeyer, Stephens, and Stephens (1992) rejected Moore's association of democracy with the bourgeoisie and argued instead that the working class (organized in unions and labor-based political parties) is the primary carrier of democracy. They see the working class as the most consistently pro-democratic class, the landed classes as the most hostile to democracy, and the bourgeoisie as inconsistent or ambiguous. For these authors, democratization occurs during capitalist economic development when the classes demanding democracy become stronger than those resisting it (Collier 1999a, 10).

Like the transitions literature, Rueschemeyer, Stephens, and Stephens acknowledged the differentiation of state institutions from the overall structure of power and wealth in society; however, these scholars sensibly asserted that, in spite of some institutional separation, the wider system of social inequality cannot be detached from the sphere of the state and the exercise of formal political power. Thus they argued that power and privilege are mutually supportive and threaten democratic institutions: "It would be foolish to overlook, for instance, that the distribution of land in El Salvador creates insolvable problems for democracy in that country. This leads to complex questions about real and formal democracy" (1992, 41).

The work of these scholars sparked a new spate of historically grounded literature exploring the role of social forces and subordinate class pressure in democratization efforts, both past and present. Collier (1999a) made the point that democratization is a resource-based process. Subordinate groups with more resources are in a better position to press for democracy. Labor union resources include organization, mobilizational capacity, and sources of power, such as votes and money. With an increase in power, the working class affected the strategies of other class actors and made them advocates of democratic reforms. While Collier did not focus on rural dynamics, it is reasonable to assume that she would consider land a central resource in the class struggles between landed classes and the peasantry.

As important as structure or class balance obviously is to democratic (or authoritarian) outcomes, the transitions literature is correct to argue that individuals make the choices that initiate regime change. Regime outcomes are most usefully understood in terms of both class and strategic perspectives—by the way they are advanced by class interests and also motivated by the strategic calculations of elites (Collier 1999a, 193–94). Foweraker (1994) and Markoff (1996) have suggested a dialogue between reforming elite insiders or power holders on the one hand and challenging mass-based movements on the other. Tarrow advocates an approach that draws attention to the "politics of the transition process, in which elites and masses, institutions and newly formed organizations interact in the context of social and institutional structures" (1995, 205). For Tarrow, actors other than elites can choose democratization (or its opposite) and follow the paths of collective action that enhance the possibility of one choice or the other.

All of these political economy arguments emphasize the importance of structure in understanding the process of democratization. To a large extent they also all view the shift of resources to labor and the peasantry as crucial to democratization, while strong landed upper classes hinder it and the bourgeoisie has a more ambiguous role. Democratic prospects are enhanced when economic inequality decreases and the balance of class power moves in favor of subordinate interests.

If we accept the argument that capitalist development contributes to democracy primarily because it develops a more beneficial class structure, then we need to pay careful attention to the content of contemporary market-oriented policies. In this light, many current marketization projects hinder democratization.

Two Approaches to Market Reforms: Neo-liberal and Shared-Growth Reforms

There is little doubt that economic and political arrangements in most of the Third World have been dramatically altered during the global implementation of market-oriented policies in the last two decades. Prior to that, import-substitution industrialization (ISI) policies supported populist coalitions that were glued together ideologically by a commitment to industrialization, nationalism (O'Donnell 1973), and (vaguely) socialism, although the policies followed by most countries of the Third World could be more accurately described as "state capitalism." These populist regimes could be democratic, but most took an authoritarian form, with political power rooted in single parties or the military.

Import-substitution policies were so called because the overarching objective of economic policies was to develop domestic manufacturing capability for goods previously imported. Such policies included import controls, overvalued exchange rates, binding ceilings on interest rates, a heavy dose of public ownership, and pervasive price regulation (Rodrik 1996). The development strategy was partly premised on the extraction of rural surplus, but agricultural policies also focused on rapidly reducing rural poverty and land concentration through government intervention. Such policies gave land to the tiller and favored group and state ownership of land, cooperatives, and land reform.

Initially, ISI policies allowed the state to become an arena for class compromise while economic strategy pursued widely popular goals of industrialization and greater economic and political independence from the advanced industrial powers. High tariff protection preserved the national market for domestic producers. Subsequently, domestic industry provided economic growth that underwrote the costs of social welfare policies. Large middle and working classes came into being and state-owned enterprises provided employment as urbanization increased. Populist leaders activated popular forces, particularly through corporate-controlled labor organizations, and included them in the political process. An uneasy alliance also developed between the protected industries and the bureaucrats administering the protection (Rodrik 1996). While urban interests prevailed over rural interests, politicians constructed broad-based populist coalitions built around the dynamic core of rapidly expanding domestic industries (O'Donnell 1973, 55).

After a period of generally high growth rates and progress in industrialization, economic stagnation or crisis initiated the demise of ISI populism. Initially, domestic light industry expanded easily and extensively and provided an engine of growth based on the easy or horizontal phase of industrialization (O'Donnell 1973). However, the deepening of industrialization, i.e., the production of intermediate and capital goods, proved to be anything but easy. Initially, the intermediate and capital goods needed for the light consumer goods industry had to be imported and paid for by the traditional agricultural exports neglected in an import substitution strategy. When these exports proved inadequate to achieve this aim, most states borrowed extensively and accumulated a heavy debt burden. This contributed to balance-of-payments crises and hyperinflation that naturally led to major political tensions. In addition, the need for higher domestic investment levels during the deepening of industrialization shook up the class compromises within ISI populism. Either the wealthy would have to be taxed at a higher rate or popular consumption would have to be reduced (Rueschemeyer, Stephens, and Stephens 1992). By the 1980s, experiencing both economic crises and severe political tensions, most countries of the Third World were forced to search for alternative economic strategies and political arrangements. Market economic reforms began to dominate the development agenda.

At least two basic approaches to economic reform are possible. Market-oriented policies in late developers typically follow what is commonly called a neo-liberal strategy or the so-called "Washington Consensus." John Williamson (1990, 1329) coined the term to summarize "the conventional wisdom of the day among the economically influential bits of Washington, meaning the US government and the international financial institutions."[4]

The neo-liberal reform model sponsored by the IMF and the World Bank comprises stabilization and structural adjustment measures. The central purpose of stabilization is to slow down inflation and improve the financial position of the state. Policies include devaluing the currency, reducing public-sector investment, and restraining consumption by keeping wage increases below the inflation rate, cutting subsidies and welfare programs, and tightening the availability of credit. The central goal of structural adjustment is to increase the efficiency of resource allocation. This is to be achieved by liberalizing trade, freeing prices, reducing the state's role in the economy, and privatizing state-owned firms. Little in the neo-liberal approach attempts to share growth during the market transition by targeting small and medium enterprises or aiding peasants and agricultural laborers with insufficient access to land and credit. The end result is a bias toward elites in urban and rural sectors. For Williamson, the Washington of the 1980s "was essentially contemptuous of equity concerns" (Williamson 1993, 1329).

Neo-liberal reforms have been the source of vociferous and often polarized debates. Some suggest that the near universal adoption of the policies in late-developing countries reflects the increasing bargaining power of the advanced industrial powers and their domestic allies, who impose the economic model in order to advance their interests.[5] An opposing camp is completely persuaded by the technical soundness of the economic blueprint and views politics, demo-

4. See also Williamson 1993 and John Williamson, "The Washington Consensus Revisited," in Louis Emmerij, ed. *Economic and Social Development into the Twenty-First Century* (Baltimore: Johns Hopkins University Press, 1997).
5. Barbara Stallings (1990) attributed a strong role to powerful domestic interests and international activities in the adoption of neo-liberal reforms. Dependency theorists such as Samir Amin (1998) have reacted to the policies of the IMF and the World Bank. Timothy Mitchell (1999) argues that the major effect of the neo-liberal program has been to concentrate public funds into different, but fewer, hands.

cratic or otherwise, as an instrument that should be used to implement "correct" economic policies made by technocrats.[6]

However, despite the polarization of the debate, there is a growing intellectual consensus on some key points. Critics of neo-liberal reforms generally accept the need for and effectiveness of neo-liberal stabilization measures once an economy has gone into an inflationary spiral, although they may find fault with sharp welfare cuts (Taylor 1991, 1999). There is also widespread acknowledgment that we do not know enough to identify appropriate structural adjustment measures for all contexts. Dani Rodrik (1996) asserts that the consensus on what constitutes appropriate structural reform is based on much shakier theoretical and empirical ground than is the consensus on the need for macroeconomic stability.

Overall, contemporary economics is not particularly strong on theories of growth, and views on this matter are both inconclusive and hotly contested (O'Donnell 1996b). Certainly the rapid economic growth rates in East Asia in the 1980s and early 1990s raised questions about an economic strategy that ruled out a significant role for state intervention.

Rodrik offers an interesting analysis of why both parts of neo-liberal reforms, stabilization and structural adjustment measures, continue to be implemented around the developing world in spite of the doubts about appropriate structural reforms. The reforms are generally implemented in a context of economic crisis. They typically follow a period of ISI policies that has culminated in economic stagnation. According to Rodrik, although most economists agreed that imprudent macroeconomic policies caused the economic crisis, they still sought to eliminate all ISI policies, because they were ideologically committed to eradicating state intervention in the economy. Economic crisis and the resulting growing power of the World Bank in determining economic policy in the developing world allowed reformist governments under the influence of orthodox economists to package macroeconomic stabilization and structural adjustment measures. The end result would be to wipe clean the entire import-substitution industrialization slate:

> The opportunity to do something that will benefit almost everyone by a large margin—stabilization, an opportunity that arises only when the economy is

6. This style of market-reform policymaking is so widespread that the contributors to Przeworski et al. 1995 view it as almost inherent in the neo-liberal approach (esp. p. 81). The literature on the political economy of adjustment focuses on implementing the reforms and devotes little attention to their impact on political development. See Nelson 1990 and Haggard and Kaufman 1992b.

mismanaged terribly and falls into deep crisis—allows reformist policy makers to sneak in, alongside the stabilization measures, microeconomic and structural reforms which have significant distributional implications and which would be difficult to implement under normal circumstances. (Rodrik 1996, 28)

The harsh criticisms of neo-liberal reforms are due in part to their tendency to forge ahead, typically in an authoritarian manner, with policies that are on shaky empirical and theoretical ground and that hold significant distributional implications. O'Donnell (1996a, 338) also makes the point that for most economists equitable growth is outside the scope of serious discussion. However, for anyone interested in the effect of economic changes on efforts to establish and consolidate democratic governance, the equity implications of market reforms are absolutely critical.

While a fuller discussion of the impact of neo-liberal reforms on poverty and equity will follow in the Tunisian case study, I can note some of the literature's broad conclusions on the politics of economic reform. With some recent challenges (Alesina 1996; Bruno, Ravallion, and Squire 1995), most studies concluded that neo-liberal reforms implemented in the 1980s hurt the poor. A major publication by authors associated with UNICEF (Cornia, Jolly, and Stewart 1987) spurred widespread demands for reform policies that would benefit the poor. Subsequently, the IMF and the World Bank incorporated many of these recommendations (Herbst 1993, 146). However, critics claimed that many of the reforms formally adopted by the Bank were never implemented and the Bank continued to focus insufficiently on the welfare of vulnerable groups.

The reforms also seem to increase an underclass concentrated in the informal sector (Nelson et al. 1994). This trend raises risks of widespread alienation that is easily exploitable by anti-democratic opportunists. Neo-liberal reforms have additionally been associated with corruption and blatant enrichment of the powerful. Rent-seeking seems common in the new market arrangements (Schamis 1999; Nelson et al. 1994). While the rich get richer, the middle strata, including civil servants and the large public service sectors, unionized industrial workers, and pensioners, are getting poorer (Nelson et al. 1994). Clearly, neo-liberal reforms reduce the political power of labor unions. Governments are retreating from their earlier roles in wage determination, and high unemployment and trade liberalization sharply reduce the power of unions to bargain with private management (Nelson et al. 1994, 24). Neo-liberal economic transformation is also associated with land redistribution upward in a number of countries, as chapter 5 of this book will detail.

On the other side of the issue, some proponents of neo-liberal reforms challenge the claims that these economic policies increase inequality or harm the poor. Bruno, Ravallion, and Squire (1995) argue that there is no systematic link between growth and inequality over time. The impact on equality is more or less neutral: high-inequality countries remain inegalitarian, while low-inequality countries, such as many of the Asian countries, remain egalitarian and rapidly reduce poverty in the process of growth. In addition, the authors assert that on average absolute poverty will fall with increased growth. Critics, they argue, are confounding the effects of economic instability and decline with the alleged effects of adjustment efforts to correct the economic problems. Far from being anti-poor, adjustment, in their view, is crucial to the welfare of the poor. The key to reduced poverty is economic growth. If growth is rapid due to neo-liberal reforms, than poverty will drop even without pro-poor measures (Nelson 1989).

Despite these conflicting views regarding the distributive effects of adjustment, the facts seem to point toward a frequent worsening of income distribution patterns. Even Bruno, Ravallion, and Squire (1995) admit that in the Philippines adverse distributional effects resulted in higher poverty rates in spite of modest growth in the late 1980s; and in Africa during the same period, overall poverty increased. In the case of Africa, macroeconomic stabilization measures (where implemented) helped the poor, but budget contractions needed to be balanced by increasing targeted social transfers to protect the poor. There is a pretty clear consensus that structural adjustment worsened income inequalities in Latin America (Chalmers et al. 1997). This is also the case in the North African countries with which I am most familiar.

In sum, the neo-liberal approach to equity and poverty issues relies on growth-led poverty reduction and targeted social transfers to the poor. Strands of this literature appear to suggest that neo-liberal policies in fact serve to reduce poverty and increase employment, and can in themselves deliver growth with equity, and that therefore social concerns are already adequately addressed by the mainstream approach (Gore 2000, 795). The reforms as currently conceived and implemented, however, clearly do not take equitable development seriously.

There is an alternative economic reform strategy that is grounded in a notion of equitable growth and that would shift the balance of class power in a direction much more favorable for democratization. Termed a "shared-growth" approach, this strategy has been distilled from the experience of East Asian countries (World Bank 1993). In a shared-growth approach leaders establish the principle of shared growth, promising that as the economy expands all groups will benefit.

First, leaders convince economic elites to support pro-growth policies. Then they persuade the elites to share the benefits of the growth with the middle class and poor. Finally, to win the cooperation of the middle class and poor, the leaders show them that they will benefit from future growth. Explicit mechanisms are used to demonstrate the commitment to share future wealth. These include comprehensive land reform, higher prices for crops produced by the small peasantry, workers' cooperatives, some housing programs, and the establishment of programs to enhance small and medium enterprise. In East Asia, this strategy was implemented under authoritarian rulers. Current mass-led and at least partially successful democratization efforts in South Korea and Taiwan bolster the argument that if subordinate groups are strengthened, then they will make the democratization push on their own.

Formal World Bank policy indeed appears to be moving toward the acceptance of an overall shared-growth approach to economic reform. The 2000–2001 *World Development Report,* devoted to attacking poverty, advocates a framework that expands economic opportunity for the poor by building up their assets and increasing the returns on these assets, through a combination of market-oriented and non-market actions. The report asserts that more equal societies can actually grow faster, dispelling the concern that greater equality would come at the expense of growth. Thus, the report advocates taking national action for a more equitable distribution of assets, including land. This means "public action is critical to ensuring secure access to land for poor people. Land reform that enhances equity and productivity is usually what first comes to mind" (World Bank 2000b, 93).[7]

Undoubtedly, the potential change in Bank policies has been spurred by popular discontent with neo-liberal reforms and a growing chorus of scholars (some working within the World Bank) advocating something that resembles a shared-growth approach to economic reform. Solimano (1999) contends that it is time to rethink the development paradigm and argues that income distribution and the reduction of social inequality are valid policy targets on their

---

7. The preliminary *World Development Report 2000/2001* was posted on the World Bank's Web site. This quotation is taken from that document. The published final report, also Web-posted, continued to stress the importance of imitating successful cases of land reform. The report indicated that such redistributive policies can also improve efficiency and growth (World Bank 2000b, vi, 56–57).

own. He advocates social policies to promote equitable development that include good, broad-based education and health services, greater access to credit for low-income households and small-scale producers, and more equal access to land and ownership of capital stock (say, after privatization). Deininger and Olinto (1999) demonstrated that across countries initial inequality in land ownership is associated with low growth. They argue that inequality in land ownership is linked to rural poverty, which limits human capital formation and thus growth. Birdsall, Graham, and Sabot (1998) acknowledge the success of macroeconomic reforms in Latin America and "aim at building a Latin consensus on a second round of reforms—reforms that would address the inequality issue without undermining efficient growth" (1998, 2). The contributors to the volume explore a range of market-friendly measures that would promote inclusive growth.

In a broader critique, Charles Gore (2000) contends that a challenge to neoliberal reforms exists in an approach that amalgamates East Asian developmentalism and Latin American neo-structuralism. Gore claims that the alternative, which he calls "the Southern consensus," offers "a different economic analysis of how growth occurs in late industrializing countries and on this basis proposes a different policy orientation to the dominant paradigm" (2000, 796). From the perspective of this postulated Southern consensus, national economic growth involves a process of catching up in which national enterprises build up production capabilities and international competitiveness in a range of activities. The approach rejects the idea that growth with late industrialization can be fostered with a standard blueprint. Policy measures have to be adapted to initial conditions and the external environment, and must change over time as the economy matures (796).

The first tenet of the approach is that growth and structural change are achieved through the "strategic integration" of the national economy into the international economy. This differs from both delinking from the rest of the world and rapidly opening up the economy across the board to imports and external capital. As far as possible, import liberalization should be gradual, to enable national enterprises to build up production capabilities and thus face external competition. Tariffs should also be complemented by measures to promote exports (797).

Second, growth and structural reform are best promoted though a combination of macroeconomic policy and "productive development policy." The macroeconomic policy is growth-oriented. It seeks to reduce inflation and fiscal deficits, but also aims to ensure full utilization of production capacity.

The productive development policy involves a range of measures designed to improve the supply capabilities of the economy, and to help private enterprise identify and acquire comparative advantage. These measures are founded on a dynamic interpretation of comparative advantage (797).

Third, the successful implementation of development policies requires government-business cooperation within the framework of a pragmatic developmental state. And, fourth, distributional dimensions of the growth process are managed in order to ensure its overall legitimacy. The main bases for a more equitable and inclusive growth process are wide asset ownership and the expansion of productive employment. Important policies include land reform, support for small and medium enterprises, and broad-based human resource development (798).

Still, in spite of this growing literature advocating a shared-growth approach to economic reform, the academic debate about appropriate market reform strategies has had little impact to date on the real world. The neo-liberal reform model continues to dominate the political agenda of late-developing countries. Little in the neo-liberal approach employs mechanisms to share growth as the economy expands.

From the standpoint of politics, even the perception of growing social inequality, linked to marketization drives, has important political implications. Politics is essentially about who gets what, when, and how (Lasswell 1936), and individuals and social groups are often politically mobilized by a sense of relative losses. Even when neo-liberal reforms promote economic growth, which in the long term mitigates trends toward inequality, intense feelings of injustice among the middle classes and poor corrode confidence in market solutions and democratic institutions (Nelson et al. 1994). In sum, in spite of alternative market-reform models, most late developers implement neo-liberal reforms that sharply aggravate socioeconomic inequalities. The political implications of these inequalities deserve serious attention in studies of economic and political change.

The Politics of Economic Reform

There is a vast literature on different aspects of market-oriented reforms, in addition to the body of writing on transitions from authoritarian to democratic political systems reviewed here, but the two trends are usually analyzed separately. They are brought together in the growing literature on the politics of economic reform, but this literature often looks only at the short term and focuses narrowly on political obstacles to the implementation of neo-liberal reforms (Nelson et al. 1994, 3). It has been criticized for judging the success of neo-liberal reforms only by their implementation or by the resumption of economic growth. The literature rarely addresses how market forces and economic policies influence political development. In most works democracy is treated as an instrumental value and the authoritarian style in which the reforms are generally implemented is implicitly sanctioned. In reaction to this, analysts have turned to the question of how to implement economic reforms under democratizing conditions (Przeworski et al. 1995).

In the last chapter of their edited volume *The Politics of Economic Adjustment*, Stephan Haggard and Robert Kaufman (1992a) explicitly explore the link between market reforms and democracy. They make a fairly strong case that the impact of market reforms on economic inequality may foster trends toward political authoritarianism in less-developed countries: "economic liberalism and political democracy may be in conflict for countries at certain stages of growth. This is due, first, to the social dislocations and increasing inequality characteristic of the early stages of development" (341). These inevitable strains are only exacerbated by market-oriented reforms and may lead to authoritarian outcomes:

> A second, and more fundamental, source of tension between capitalism and democracy in the Third World resides in the nature of the social structure. Highly inequitable distributions of assets and income, and particularly severe rural inequalities, pose threats to stability. Thus while all democratic political systems face the tension between stratified societies and open politics, these tensions are likely to be acute in the developing world, increasing the likelihood of either revolutionary or reactionary political outcomes. (342)

Curiously, the authors do not proceed to use a framework that links actor choice to social structure in their exploration of the relationship between regime type and the development of a market-oriented economy. Instead, the analysis follows the dominant trend in the democratization literature by focusing on the institutionalization of political parties by political elites as the variable that largely determines the consolidation of democratic rule. A later work by Haggard and Kaufman (1995) does go somewhat further in integrating economic circumstances into the analysis of regime change. In this work, democratic consolidation largely depends on two factors. First, market reforms need to be implemented in order to improve economic performance (indeed, the authors come close to saying that this should initially be done in an authoritarian manner, followed by a gradual reduction of executive power). Second, the authors continue to emphasize the importance of party systems in successful transitions to market economies and democratic politics. In essence, they focus on how the distributive consequences of market reforms can be contained by representative institutions; the coalition politics that they consider to be at the heart of the politics of adjustment emphasize the need to "control" those who lose in economic reform.

Haggard and Kaufman's perspective on the politics of economic adjustment is worth exploring further because it reflects a neo-classical understanding of economic reform convincingly challenged by Hector Schamis (1999). The neo-classical political economy approach has explained ISI state-intervention as the result of the deliberate action of distributional coalitions—rent seekers who profit from subsidies, tariffs, and regulations. According to the neo-classical perspective, a liberal economic order is a public good that requires heroic policy-makers who are willing to launch policies that abolish the privileges of powerful and well-organized interest groups while often facing economic crisis and political instability. One of the puzzles of the scope, pace, and length of the liberalization trend (in some countries, over twenty years) is how policymakers managed to overcome such an unfavorable context for collective action and make considerable progress in the implementation of neo-liberal reforms. The literature on the politics of economic adjustment explains the success of reforming elites by focusing on the resolve and insulation of policymakers, who implement the reforms in an authoritarian manner and who politically manage groups that favor the status quo, by either compensating them, obfuscating the intent of the policy, or perhaps repressing them.

The politics of economic adjustment literature asserts that economic liberalization concentrates present costs on the beneficiaries of ISI and disperses (initially uncertain) benefits into the future. The losers have incentives to engage in collective action but prospective winners, facing uncertainty about payoffs, remain disorganized. The pro-reform coalition is thus seen as more fragile than those forces favoring import-substitution industrialization (Schamis 1999).

Schamis challenged the view of the politics of economic adjustment as the politics of neutralizing the losers. Instead he treats it as the politics of empowering the winners. By examining the economic reform process in Latin America, he discovered that the state most capable of launching policy reforms and sustaining them over time is the one that has become the agent of powerful economic groups. This suggests that the influence of winners and their capacity for collective action have offset the power of the losers. Policymaking elites insulated themselves from the losers by forming alliances with groups of beneficiaries who were well informed about the payoffs of the reforms before they were implemented. From these links, reformist governments drew organized political support for economic liberalization.

Furthermore, Schamis argues that the Latin American experience demonstrates that the coalitions that organized in support of liberalization are most appropriately described as distributional. "The ties policymakers built with the firms that benefited from the process account for collusion; and the behavior engaged in by interest groups in order to reap the benefits of state withdrawal can be adequately defined as rent seeking" (Schamis 1999, 238).

Clientelism: The Revival of a Pernicious Partial Regime

Clearly, there is reason to seriously question the widespread notion that markets foster democracy. In fact, neo-liberal economic transitions potentially threaten democratic prospects in a number of areas. It is easier to understand the link between economic reform and political change if we disaggregate the process. I suggest modifying Schmitter's (1992, 1995) disaggregated approach to democratic consolidation. Schmitter writes,

> What if modern democracy were conceptualized not as "a regime," but as a composite of partial regimes, each of which was institutionalized around distinctive sites for the representation of social groups and the resolution of their ensuing conflicts? Parties, associations, movements, localities, and various clientele would compete and coalesce around these different channels in [order to advance their interests] and influence policy. . . . [Variances in civil society concern] the power resources that actors can bring to bear on the emerging political process. (1992, 160, 162)

Since new channels of representation for social groups can emerge in new authoritarian regimes as well as new democratic ones, it can be useful to consider how neo-liberal reforms affect the partial regimes that Schmitter lists, without any teleological focus on democratization. He lists the concertation regime, in which the government, organized labor, and capital cooperate in policymaking (this concept is linked to earlier descriptions of societal and state corporatism); the electoral regime; the pressure regime, dominated by interest groups and other associations in civil society; and the clientelistic regime.

This book demonstrates how, in the Tunisian case, market-oriented reforms enhanced a pernicious partial regime—clientelism. Landed elites (and the bourgeoisie) formed the core of the new authoritarian regime. Facing an invigorated landlord class, peasants turned to clientelism and withdrew from formal political institutions. Agricultural unions became the exclusive domain of rural notables. Similarly weakened in urban areas, the national labor union, which had led the democracy movement, accommodated a new authoritarian order and agreed to new state corporatist arrangements.

These developments make sense if our elite-centered, process-oriented understanding of regime transitions is joined by a more realistic appreciation of the political implications of socioeconomic inequality and institutional constraints. Given the nature of neo-liberal economic reforms, it is not surprising that new political coalitions of the powerful emerge in the new political arrangements, and that they may undermine democratic prospects. Dominant party regimes like Tunisia may abandon their populist orientation, but they also have mechanisms of social control (developed party structures) with which they can retain power during economic crisis or development (Haggard and Kaufman 1992a). Institutional legacies may be more important than the introduction of superficial new processes and institutions by political leaders formally committing a country to democracy.

Highly unequal distributions of assets and incomes, particularly in rural areas, hinder democratization. The more unequal the social structure, the more likely are authoritarian outcomes. The more political, organizational, and economic resources available to labor and the peasantry, the better the chance that they will be able to address the problems they face and serve as agents of democracy. To the degree that market-oriented reforms hinder collective organization by these subordinate groups, they likely hinder democratic prospects.

NEO-LIBERAL TRANSFORMATION IN TUNISIA

Neo-liberal transformation in Tunisia accentuated a growing alliance between the state and rural and urban economic elites. During Tunisia's period of state-led, inward-oriented growth (1961–69), the state was arguably autonomous. In its pursuit of industrialization and agrarian modernization, the bureaucratic establishment and leaders of the country's single political party often undertook policies that advanced state elite desires for rapid modernization and greater social equity even when those aims conflicted with the interests of powerful social groups (Zghal 1973; King 1998). However, even during Tunisia's "socialist" phase, a period when the political elite's will to transform society was at its height, the state's relative autonomy and commitment to its own developmental agenda were tempered in two ways. First, the state party's leadership came from rural areas and the party was initially funded by rural notables (Anderson 1986; Hermassi 1972); thus the post-independence policy process has frequently reflected the state's vulnerability to the vested interests of rural elites. Second, state patronage and state policy were used to create a populist authoritarian political order, as well as to pursue modernization.

Even during the socialist or statist era, development policy in rural areas, which in some developing countries aggressively sought to reduce land concentration and rural poverty, remained tepid in Tunisia. Rich colonial farms that had been converted into state lands were turned into agricultural production cooperatives administered by the state and tilled by landless laborers and the small peasantry. In the pre-colonial era these had been feudal or landlord estates, with property rights contested by rural notables tied to the Ottoman beylical regime and the tenant cultivators of the lands. These coveted farms did not go to the rural gentry in the early post-independence era; neo-liberal economic polices in the late 1980s and 1990s achieved this multigenerational goal. Redistributive land reform of Tunisian private property, necessary for the success of agricultural production cooperatives, also did not occur.

During the period of gradual economic liberalization (1970–86), state policy shifted to a (re-)commitment to a private sector along with the state and co-operative sectors. The state began to evince more of a bias toward economic elites. Using their special ties with the political leadership, the rural gentry began to encroach on state lands and to take advantage of state policy to transform themselves into an urban bourgeoisie:

> Not a few of these entrepreneurs [a new commercial bourgeoisie] had been provincial landowners, and they had accumulated capital in the agricultural sector . . . and increased their productivity through mechanization. They also diversified their investments beyond commercial agriculture to transport, construction, and hotel management. Partly because of the continued significance of patronage, they enjoyed easy, often preferential, access to government and private credit. It was they who would profit from economic liberalization and Bourguiba was to give them the opportunity in the 1970s. (Anderson 1986, 240)

The 1970s and 1980s in Tunisia were decades of major socioeconomic changes and severe political conflict. Mass mobilization sparked demands for political liberalization and electoral competition. Unsuccessful transitions to a national democratic regime were initiated in 1981 and again in 1987. President Ben Ali (1987–present) accelerated neo-liberal transformation in Tunisia. During his tenure, initiatives toward broad-based political competition at the national level appear to have culminated in a hegemonic party system and the revitalization of state corporatism. Rural elites and their urban offshoot form the core coalition of this new authoritarian order, and largely determine the state's economic projects.

To a degree, rural areas have been isolated from Tunisia's experiments in multipartyism. The highly clientelistic organization of agriculture and the alliance between rural notables and state elites have perpetuated authoritarian control of the countryside, even while peasants have been drawn into participation in formal political institutions (Anderson 1986, 249). The recent accelerated free-market modernization of the rural sector in Tunisia, however, produced even more extreme imbalances in rural social power (see below and chapter 4). Rural workers and peasants face even greater hurdles to the development of autonomous organizations for interest aggregation and political expression. This chapter argues that market economic reforms in Tunisia subverted emerging democratic tendencies in the country. The following two chapters explore how the revitalization of cultural traditionalism in rural communities helps to sustain this new authoritarian order.

The Collapse of ISI Populism and
Demands for Democratic Contestation

Since independence in 1956, Tunisian politics have been dominated by an authoritarianism whose central pillar has been a hegemonic political party that has shifted names and ideological orientation over time (Neo-Destour, Socialist Destour, Rally for Constitutional Democracy). This single-party state has used corporatist strategies to organize political interests and power (Richards and Waterbury 1996; Murphy 1999). Although the national labor union (UGTT) has at times been independent, Tunisian corporatism has tended toward state authoritarianism rather than societal corporatism, in which the organic community is built on a more consensual partnership between state and society (Schmitter 1979). Tunisia's first post-independence president, Habib Bourguiba, built a powerful state apparatus (borrowing key cadres from his party) to supplement the Neo-Destour in the construction of this authoritarian political system. In a centralized system that spread to every urban and rural district, high-ranking party personnel so dominated governmental offices that influence in reality was confined to a relatively small regime elite (Moore 1965).

The post-independence state project in Tunisia took shape in the 1960s. Changing its name to Socialist Destour, the party embarked on the path of rapid state-led modernization. State-administered agricultural production cooperatives built around confiscated foreign holdings were the centerpiece of the strategy (Simmons 1970). The state also stepped in as the major industrial investor in the early years after independence. The reforms of the economy also encompassed regulation of industry, commerce, prices, and credit (Waterbury and Richards 1996). Government enterprises served as a model for private entrepreneurs to emulate. Public enterprises stimulated the private sector through backward and forward linkages to other industries (Harik 1992, 211). Jobs were created for the growing urban labor force, especially in the public sector. On the negative side, a large resource gap was created when the country tried to invest more resources than were saved domestically. The gaps were filled for the most part by borrowing from abroad (Waterbury and Richards 1996, 206). The Socialist Destour also took on a heavy burden of welfare provision that helped build the populist coalition (Harik 1992, 212).

In the most proximate sense, the collapse of ISI populism in Tunisia was due to events in the agricultural sector. Despite fairly widespread discontent with the agricultural cooperatives, the minister of planning, Ahmed Ben Salah, attempted to further cooperativize the economy. However, large landholders led a protest in 1969 that culminated in Ben Salah's ouster and a state policy shift toward economic liberalization. This major shift in policy meant the end of Tunisian socialism. The collapse of the cooperative movement also meant the failure of the first major effort by the Tunisian government to deliver on the promises of the struggle for independence. Demands for political liberalization and electoral competition began within this context.

The analysis of failed democratization and the relatively slow implementation of a new form of authoritarian rule in Tunisia must address at least three issues. Why was a process of democratization set in motion at all, and what individual or collective actors began it? Once it was underway, what determined its direction? And was the final outcome (in this case the abortion of the process and the reconfiguration of authoritarianism) inevitable (Whitehead 1986)?

Two factors provided the opportunity for elite and mass mobilization for regime change in Tunisia. The first was the shift in economic policy toward a greater reliance on market forces (although reduced cooperative and state sectors still remained) and the second was the difficulty of maintaining broad-based support in the authoritarian political system due to the regime's disavowal of socialism and apparent growing inattention to popular concerns.

Labor. Tunisia's economic reorientation made it more difficult for the UGTT's leadership to keep the rank and file behind the regime. Negotiations over wages, benefits, and working conditions eventually evolved into militant challenges of the single-party system, and these militants set in motion the process of democratization probably more than any other actor, individual or collective. Economic setbacks and abuses of labor codes by management and owners sparked an outbreak of rank-and-file unrest in 1969 that gained strength in 1971–72 (Alexander 1996, 182).

The government attempted to quell the unrest and reestablish UGTT support through the instrument of a new collective bargaining system (instituted in 1973) that made the UGTT an equal partner with the business union (Union Tunisienne de l'Industrie, du Commerce et de l'Artisanat, UTICA) and the state. The new bargaining arrangements raised wages and provided a wide range of additional bonuses and indemnities, but the measures failed to provide the social peace that the government wanted. In fact, the number of strikes increased steadily. Rising worker militancy stemmed largely from relative losses suffered by workers. "The economic analysis prepared by the UGTT's 1977 congress showed that inflation rose 36 percent between 1970 and 1977, while real wages had risen only 7 percent. . . . The union argued that although the Tunisian economy was growing, the government's policies did not divide the growth equitably" (Alexander 1996, 182). Economic downturn in the late 1970s accentuated these grievances.

Organized labor, more than any elite or other collective actors, led the demand for a democratic opening in Tunisia. Major clashes pitted the UGTT against the single-party regime:

> They [the new UGTT leadership] argued that improving workers' conditions was not simply a matter of influencing policy within the confines of the ruling party. Rather, it required defining specific working class interests and defending them against other, antagonistic class interests. As these more politicized unionists rose to positions of influence over the course of the 1970s, they expanded the UGTT's agenda to include calls for democratic reform and other explicitly political demands. (Alexander 1996, 183)

Students. Student organizations also responded to the 1969 rupture in the political system. At the same time that labor began its strikes and demonstrations, student groups organized strikes at the universities. Some government officials feared that a new radical opposition movement was trying to unite students and workers (Alexander 1996, 182). Student groups also joined a general strike called by the UGTT on January 26, 1978. This strike descended into violence.

Fundamentalists. As elsewhere in the Arab world, an Islamist movement has mobilized the population against an entrenched authoritarian regime. In the Tunisian case, perhaps more than any other, the Islamist leadership, throughout most of its history, has also asserted its adherence to democratic principles. Most analysts trace the emergence of Tunisia's Islamist movement to the same 1969–70 collapse of Tunisian socialism that helped spur a rising militant labor movement (Hamdi 1998; Anderson 1986, 246; Hermassi 1991). At the very least, the timing of the fundamentalist reaction indicates that Tunisia's Islamic movement emerged and operated within the context of the same struggle over limited resources that provoked the confrontation between the regime and labor during economic liberalization. The Islamic movement in independent Tunisia was founded as al-jama'a al-Islamiyya (the Islamic group).

> The first cell was set up in 1970. At that time, Tunisia was embarking on a new era of economic liberalism after the failure of the socialist experiment led by Ahmad Ben Salah. . . . The change from the co-operative socialism of Ben Salah to the economic liberalism of Hedi Nouira led to an ideological and identity crisis. (Hamdi 1998, 7)

The Islamist movement grew steadily during the 1970s, but still lacked the labor movement's power to mobilize politically and press for regime change

during the critical period in January 1978 when the UGTT and students insti-
gated a national strike that led to Black Thursday, or "the uprising." At this
point, concerned about labor's rising power, the Islamists became more radi-
calized against the regime and sought common cause with unions. They shifted
from condemning the government primarily for anti-Islamic policies to a comprehensive theological, political, and social view that "condemned the regime's
dictatorship, alliance with foreign powers, Westernization, and exploitation"
(Hamdi 1998, 32).

Regime Elites. Contrary to propositions in the democratic transitions and
consolidation literatures, elites within the regime did not create a political
opening that sparked the demands for the political liberalization of Tunisia's
single-party system. Instead it is more likely that social mobilization from below induced some elites to move toward democracy while increasing the resolve
of others to harden the authoritarian regime. In the early stages of the break
from Tunisian socialism, two unofficial parties were formed by Socialist Destour party members. Ahmed Ben Salah, himself the architect of the cooperative movement, formed the Mouvement de l'Unité Populaire (MUP), which he
led from exile in Europe, and another higher-level party official, Ahmed Mes-
tiri, organized the Mouvement des Démocrates Socialistes (MDS). However,
these opposition figures were pushed outside the state party, and the parties
they created never gained the popular support of the UGTT, or of the Islamists,
for that matter.

The presence of new unofficial political parties, an opposition Islamist
movement, and a labor movement confrontationally demanding social equity
and democratization provided clear evidence in the late 1970s that Bourguiba's
political edifice was in shambles. Observers described the once populist authoritarian regime as declining "into atrophy, centralization, authoritarianism,
and corruption. The exclusion of progressive, leftist, and democratic tendencies left it weakened in an increasingly heterogeneous and conflict-ridden political environment" (Tessler, White, and Entelis 1995, 429).

Disaggregating Authoritarian Reconfiguration:
The Electoral Regime

President Habib Bourguiba did not survive the clashes between state and
society. His government reneged on a multiparty experiment in 1981. Bourguiba was aging and showing signs of senility, and his ministerial decisions and
personal conduct became erratic. State trials and planned executions of his

bête noire, the Islamists, led the country to the brink of civil war. On November 7, 1987, General Ben Ali, a former strongman for the regime who had recently been appointed prime minister, implemented a bloodless coup and came to power pledging a commitment to democracy and accelerated market economic reforms.[1] Under Ben Ali, national democratization appeared to commence on the correct footing. In 1988, the new president convinced the leaders of the country's main social forces to sign a national pact. In it they pledged to end the single-party system, the marginalization of institutions, the personalization of power, and the monopolization of authority.[2] The democratic transitions literature considers this pact crucial. Tunisia's democratic hopes were also bolstered by a political culture widely regarded as being more conducive to democratic governance than perhaps any of the other Arab states of the Middle East and North Africa. Trends in political culture were supplemented by a century-long legacy of constitutional rule making and political reform.

Ben Ali implemented new processes and institutions to restore equilibrium in the system. The steps he took fit the transitions literature's institutional benchmarks for an elite-led democratic transition. However, the changes have not penetrated deeply enough or functioned well enough to sustain a democratic allocation of power.[3] The regime experimented with a multiparty political system. Ben Ali renamed his Socialist Destour the Rassemblement Constitutionnel Démocratique (RCD). The state party spawned spin-offs to contest "foundational" legislative elections held in 1989. The MDS was reorganized to contest the elections. Other secular opposition parties included the Union Démocratique Unioniste (UDU), the Parti Social Libéral (PSL), the Rassemblement Socialiste Progressiste (RSP), and the Tunisian Communist party. However, none of these parties was able to generate popular support. The largest, the MDS, won less than 4 percent of the vote nationwide (Anderson 1990). Due to a winner-take-all electoral structure, the RCD won every open seat in the Tunisian parliament in those elections (Denoeux 1994).

The party system that Ben Ali appears to have in mind is a form of consensual authoritarianism in which the opposition is allowed to present alternative

1. On this period see Murphy 1999, Zartman 1991.
2. On the first few years of the Ben Ali presidency and the country's national pact, see Lisa Anderson, "Tunisia's National Pact in Comparative Perspective" (paper presented at a Tunisia Day conference, School of Advanced International Studies, Johns Hopkins University, 1989), and Anderson 1991.
3. This is common in developing countries undergoing economic and political change. See Olcott and Ottaway 1999 and O'Donnell 1994.

views without any prospect of significantly affecting the hegemonic role of the RCD. In public speeches the president tends to emphasize the state-led creation of multiparty politics and a civil society that does not challenge the "national consensus." In practice this has meant that the president and his advisors, along with the revitalized state party, continue to define the national consensus and remain the chief architects of state policy.

The Islamists emerged as the only challenge to RCD hegemony in the electoral arena. In his early years in power, Ben Ali vacillated on whether or not to legalize the Mouvement de la Tendance Islamique (MTI), but in the end he allowed it to run on independent lists in the 1989 elections. The government prohibited the use of the words "Islam" or "Islamic" in the name of political parties, so the MTI renamed itself the Parti de la Renaissance, or al-Nahda. The independent lists officially won almost 14 percent of the vote nationwide and up to 25 percent in large cities (Denoeux 1994, 49). Many believe that the level of support for al-Nahda was even higher.

The 1989 elections were an embarrassment for the regime's democratic pretensions, prompting it to tinker with the electoral structure for the 1994 legislative and presidential elections. The regime tailored the election law to reconcile the rhetoric of democracy with a parliament consisting entirely of members of the RCD. The changes allowed some opposition in the parliament but still ensured RCD hegemony; 19 of the 163 seats in the Chamber of Deputies were reserved for opposition political parties according to the percentage of votes they received nationwide, except for al-Nahda, which had been banned and harshly repressed by this time. The other 144 seats were allocated by a plurality system that virtually assured seats to the official party. Seven opposition parties were legally recognized and the 19 reserved seats were awarded to four of them. The MDS won ten deputy spots, the Mouvement de la Rénovation, or Ettajdid (formerly the communist party), four, the UDU three, and the Parti de l'Unité Populaire (PUP) two (Denoeux 1994).

In the legislative elections of October 1999, Ben Ali continued to "grant" a small number of seats to the opposition to maintain the façade of democracy. The opposition's presence in the Chamber of Deputies was increased to 20 percent of the total. By this time it had become evident that the legal opposition parties still did not have a significant social base of support. The RCD won over 97 percent of the total vote (EIU 1999), and even before the elections began, the results were hardly in doubt. The regime knew in advance that it would receive 80 percent of the seats. The RCD won all of the seats contested under the first-past-the-post system and the opposition parties together tallied far less than

20 percent of the national total. Thirteen seats were awarded to the MDS, seven to the PUP, five to the Ettajdid Movement, and two to the PSL (EIU 1999). In a similar vein, for the 2000 municipal elections, President Ben Ali announced that opponents would receive at least 20 percent of the municipal seats, regardless of the results of the elections (Freedom House 1999); and indeed the final count resulted in an 80/20 split. All of the legal opposition parties function as satellites to the RCD. The tiny parties recognize their weakness by characterizing themselves as parties of support, not parties of opposition (Zartman 1991, 26).

During the 1999 elections, the presidency was (nominally) contested for the first time. One analyst, to the puzzlement of some (including me), called the 1999 Tunisian presidential elections "a watershed in Arab politics between the autocratic rule of the past and the new politics of pluralism" (Fandy 1999). The heads of two minor political parties were allowed to run for president according to specific changes to the constitution that in effect allowed an incumbent president to handpick his challengers (Labidi 1999). Ben Ali's opponents were Mohammed Belhadj Amor of the PUP and Abderrahmen Tlili of the UDU. The incumbent president won 99.4 percent of the vote (EIU 1999).

More than specific political programs and ideology, the opposition presidential candidates have complained of bureaucratic control over electoral politics and presidential domination of the political system. Tlili voiced concern about equal financing opportunities for all candidates during the campaign and neutrality of the administration during the election. Other demands included an executive more responsible to lawmakers, a more independent judicial system, and the creation of an independent council to monitor human rights in Tunisia (Daoud 1999).

Amor campaigned for strict control of the executive branch by the parliament and the establishment of another legislative chamber to allow wider representation of the various national organizations and institutions. He also called for term limits for the presidency (a maximum of two) and advocated separating the Constitutional Council from the executive branch. Both candidates complained about the lack of press freedom in the country and echoed all of the opposition parties' desire for a proportional representation system so that party and state could be disentangled (Daoud 1999). Even though the two candidates combined received less than one percent of the vote and still considered their parties to be supporting the regime, the issues they raised at least indicated some steps that need to be taken if multipartyism and pluralism will ever have a chance in the Tunisian setting.

The Concertation or State Corporatist Partial Regime

Economic crisis and the neo-liberal reforms that Ben Ali intensified as soon as he took power decreased the power resources that labor could bring to bear on the emerging political process (Payne 1991). Union leaders became more willing to cooperate with business and the government as their own economy became more dependent on market forces and Tunisian enterprises began to reorient themselves to compete internationally. The UGTT leadership redefined the organization's interests to accept wage moderation and a greater concern for the interests of privately owned enterprises, although many of the rank and file felt betrayed by the sacrifices that their leadership was demanding (Alexander 1996, 190).

> Our union . . . has chosen in principle to adapt itself to international transformations by adopting new methods of work and intervention. . . . Today, the union is trying to adapt to changes in the international economic system, the structural adjustment program, the new world order and the market economy. The task of meeting these challenges is the union's preoccupation. (quoted in Alexander 1996, 177)

The union rank and file, throughout the process, have maintained more radical views on these issues than union leaders, leaving open the possibility of a debilitating split between leadership and base. However, beginning in 1989, the UGTT began participating in new corporatist institutions that supported economic reform. Major agreements between the state, the UGTT, and the business association (UTICA) were signed in 1990 and 1993 to adapt Tunisian corporatism to the demands of a more market-oriented economy (Alexander 1996, 186–95). Labor moved from broad demands for democratization and economic justice to supporting corporatist arrangements and accepting a distinction between politics (pressure for democratic reforms) and trade unionism. In the end, the UGTT leadership determined that the union should remain allied with the state party, even though the party was markedly tilting toward supporting the interests of business and commercial farmers. The regime's subordination of the labor movement largely foreclosed the possibility of the birth of a labor party with a social base of support and a socialist program. Such a party, and a split in the RCD, had long been considered the main potential sources of multipartyism (Zartman 1991, 26).

The Politics of Economic Adjustment:
Empowering the Winners

The acceleration of market reforms and the subjugation of Tunisia's once powerful labor movement under Ben Ali call into question the assumed ability of the rent-seeking losers of economic reform to take collective action (Nelson 1989; Haggard and Webb 1994: Haggard and Kaufman 1992b). The regime has found its strongest support among rural and urban economic elites.

The introduction (or acceleration) of the neo-liberal project in Tunisia involved property rights reforms. Reforms of property rights are among the most important transmission mechanisms linking neo-liberal reforms to income distribution (Scott 1996, 155). The most striking instance of the state's redistributing property rights among private agents was the agrarian counter-reform. In 1968, when Tunisia's agricultural cooperatives were at their height, state farms controlled 40 percent of the nation's cultivable land, a total of 1,078,000 hectares. More than 1.5 million people lived on this land, 50 percent of the rural population (Simmons 1970, 51). During Tunisia's period of gradual economic liberalization (1970–86), a new phase began with the return of private land to owners and the ceding of some state land to private ownership. Land policy in this period amounted to distributing the lion's share of privatized land to large landowners, while preserving a small percentage of farmland for small peasants to support their families (Radwan, Jamal, and Ghose 1991, 40–41). In addition, many of the smallholders who retrieved their land in 1970 eventually lost it to large landowners; having taken out loans to resume private production, they became indebted to wealthier farmers and could no longer sustain their farms (Zamiti 1970, 52–53).

In 1985, just before structural adjustment began, 600,000 hectares were still held by the state in various forms (table 1). The state, with the support of World Bank agricultural sector loans, began managing its lands in a new way.[4] The land would be privatized in twenty-five- to forty-year leasing contracts, at rates far lower than market prices. Private investors participating in the program were also provided with credit support and technological assistance. At a later date state policy is supposed to move toward outright private ownership.[5]

4. The program actually began in 1982, but proceeded slowly until a national consultation on the issue in 1990.
5. Director of the Ministry of State Lands, interviewed by the author.

Table 1. Total Acreage in Tunisia by Property Type, 1985

Property Type	Hectares
Forest	1,240,000
State and Pilot Farms	210,000
State Teaching Farms	170,000
State Land Ceded to Private Owners	216,000
Agricultural Production Cooperatives	220,000
Communal Land	2,700,000
Land Under Private Title	4,500,000

Source: World Bank 1995a, annex C.3, 6.

For the most part, the shift in land policy has meant the cession of all state lands to large landowners, without consideration for the small peasantry as before.[6] This policy has been aggressively pursued since a 1990 national consultation on the issue. According to officials, the state wanted to maintain large parcels and guarantee investment on this land. Judging from interviews I conducted at the local and state level, it appears that they deemed large holdings to be the most productive and large landowners to be the most capable producers. State officials held this opinion in spite of an extensive literature indicating that smaller holdings are more productive than larger ones (Cassen 1994; Lipton 1977; Berry and Cline 1979). The data from Tunisia indicate that smaller-scale farms produce more per unit of land, just as they do elsewhere in the developing world (El-Ghonemy 1990). In addition, even prior to the 1990 acceleration of land privatization, wealthy farmers (those already possessing a hundred hectares of land) increased their share of total farmland from 22.9 percent in 1986 to 28.1 percent in 1989 (World Bank 1991b, 6).

Even the World Bank acknowledged that Tunisia's recent land policy worsened inequality and poverty, although the blame for the reforms' structure, which benefits the most powerful, appears to lie with the Tunisian government:

> Allocation of state-owned land and collective land to private title holders is occurring, with at best neutral, and probably negative consequences for the poor. The government is pursuing a policy of increasing productivity and promoting modern, commercial farming, on the 0.8 million hectares of land that it owns. In the last several years the government has been more aggressively

6. Agricultural technicians, usually from the Ministry of Agriculture, received special access to the few small lots available for lease.

pursuing leasing state-owned crop lands to private commercial partnerships for up to 40 years. Although there may be some indirect benefits to the rural poor from this transfer of management, the government is expressly not distributing these lands to improve the land assets of the rural poor. (World Bank 1995b, vol. 2, annex C.3, 7)

A second process of asset redistribution has been the sale of state-owned enterprises. The government privatized approximately sixty companies between 1987 and 1997 (Department of State 2000). Many more companies are scheduled for privatization in the near future. State policy regarding state-owned enterprises has benefited the wealthy in the same manner as land policy (Harik 1992, 218–19). In general, attractive incentives are offered to Tunisians who can invest capital in export industries and establish joint ventures with foreign concerns. The end result of this policy orientation is that the benefits of economic reform have accrued primarily to an elite (Payne 1991, 148). At the same time, virtually none of the small enterprises in the country's large informal sector benefit from the government's supportive and incentive measures, especially those that make credit available (World Bank 1995b, vol. 2, annex C.2). The informal sector is defined as comprising small family enterprises with no regular employees, and micro-enterprises employing no more than ten employees in manufacturing and services and five in commerce. The informal sector is neglected by state policy, although it represents, according to the latest available survey, 40 percent of non-agricultural employment and 95 percent of all enterprises (World Bank 1995b, vol. 2, annex C.2). Ironically, the World Bank credits small enterprises in the informal sector with making the biggest contribution to manufacturing gains of any group during the structural adjustment period (World Bank 1995b, vol. 2, annex C.2).

Despite an economic reform strategy sharply biased toward elites, the Tunisian government and the World Bank view the process in the country as a case of equitable growth (World Bank 1996). Neo-liberal reforms in Tunisia, to an extent, met the country's need for economic reform and partially achieved the aims of the IMF and the World Bank (Pfiefer 1999, 23–27). Budget deficits were reduced and inflation curbed (although it had never reached the hyperinflation seen in some Latin American countries). Production for export was stimulated and external account deficits and debt service were reduced, at least relative to the crisis years. The austerity programs of the early stabilization phase intensified recessionary conditions, after which macroeconomic growth was eventually restored (table 2).

Table 2. Tunisia: Growth Rate of Per Capita GDP

1970–80	*1981–1986*	*1987–1994*	*1995–2000*
4.1%	1.15%	2.44%	8%

Sources: for 1981–86 and 1987–94, World Bank 1996, 48; for 1970–80 and 1995–2000, IMF 2001.

However, in addition to concentrating assets through the property rights reforms, neo-liberalism in Tunisia likely increased inequality by not directly addressing unemployment and the deterioration of wages. The unemployment data during the reform process are alarming, with the official unemployment rate increasing from 13.1 percent in 1984 to 16.1 percent in 1993 (World Bank 1995a, vol. 1, ii). Many analysts estimate actual unemployment to be much higher (Murphy 1999, 156). Furthermore, the rate at which the labor force is growing, the acceleration of privatization, and the expected increase in dependence on extremely competitive European markets mean that the unemployment problem may be intractable. The problem will not be resolved by neo-liberal reforms stimulating private investment, growth, and new job opportunities, unless both rhetoric and practice also focus on unemployment and investment in human development (Pfiefer 1999, 27). In addition, the failure to create jobs quickly enough to absorb new entrants to the labor market has been partially disguised by the growth of the unmeasured informal sector (Pfiefer 1999; Murphy 1999, 156).

In addition to losing jobs, workers have faced a decline in wages during the economic reform process. Average wages declined in real terms 11 percent during 1983–93, with sharp declines during 1986–88. "Based on available data for 1983–93, the average real wage declined in all sectors. Clearly, this indicates that the purchasing power of wage earners, and more specifically minimum wage earners, deteriorated during the period" (World Bank 1995b, vol. 2, annex C.1).

Tunisia's record of economic reform, with both resumed macroeconomic growth and sharply inequitable structural reforms, has resulted in contestation of the level of overall inequality during the neo-liberal transformation. The two most commonly used measures of income inequality are the Gini coefficient, which looks at the disparity between equal and actual distribution of income among quintile shares, and the proportion of income received by the top 20 percent of the population (Beer 1999, 6). The Gini coefficient has been extensively critiqued on both methodological and theoretical fronts (Braun 1991; Beer 1999). In particular, the income levels of the bottom 20 percent of

Table 3. Size Distribution of Income (Percentage Share of Household Income)

Year	Lowest 20%	Second quintile	Third quintile	Fourth quintile	Highest 20%
1970/75	6.0	9.0	20.0	23.0	42.0
1990	5.9	10.4	15.3	22.1	46.3

Sources: World Bank 1994; Deininger and Squire, 1996.

any population rarely vary, so the difference between the concentration in the top percentiles and the Gini score is due almost entirely to the distribution in the middle. On the other hand, the use of upper proportional shares of income has been argued to indirectly measure asset inequality, another significant dimension of economic stratification (Boswell and Dixon 1993). Thus, clearly the appropriate measure for income inequality during economic reform is shares of income, with a particular focus on the proportion received by the top 20 percent.

Unfortunately, the available data on inequality in Tunisia (and most of the Arab world) are scanty indeed. Both the Gini coefficients and the quintile share data found in World Bank documents (including World Development Reports) and United Nations Development Programme reports have been derived from household surveys of living standards carried out, in principle, every five years by the Tunisian Institut National de la Statistique (INS). The last survey was made in 1995–96. The available pre- and post-reform figures (the latter actually dating from during the course of the reforms), including the latest data on shares of income, are collected and presented in table 3. Judging by household income, income inequality is deepening in Tunisia.

As a disturbing footnote to any effort to measure income distribution, apparently the Tunisian government has decided not to release either Gini coefficients or quintile share figures gathered from the 1995–96 household consumption surveys. The survey covered the years 1990–95, when the most substantial structural reforms (with all of their distributional implications) were implemented. Even the World Bank, which has contributed to financing the surveys, has been unable to obtain this information from Tunisian officials, "who have been more unwilling to provide indicators of inequality and poverty in the last few years."[7] The data provided by the Tunisian government to the World Bank in 1999 focused on aggregate macroeconomic statistics and eschewed indicators

7. The quotation and subsequent analysis in this paragraph are from my interview with Seterah Razmara, the contact for the World Bank's Poverty Monitoring Database.

of inequality. The reasonable implication is that inequality increased in Tunisia during economic reform to the extent that it is an embarrassment to the government, which has therefore not provided new data on this vital area in over a decade. Instead the Tunisian government and the World Bank continue to focus on aggregate growth rates and income distribution during the first few years of the reform program (World Bank 1996).

Market Reforms and the Dismantlement of the Pressure Regime

Neo-liberalism in Tunisia, as elsewhere, has been facilitated by a harsh restriction of political rights (Mitchell 1999, 32). In his first year in office, President Ben Ali inaugurated a wave of reforms that contributed to his early credentials as a democratizer. The most important were the closing of the state security court, which Bourguiba had used against the Islamists and others in the opposition; the adoption of a liberal press law; and the granting of amnesty to hundreds of political prisoners (Vandewalle 1989, 3). However, in the past decade the regime has effectively repressed virtually all of civil society.

The ratcheting up of state repression began with the Islamist movement. After al-Nahda's success in the 1989 elections, security and military concerns dominated the regime's approach to the party. (At this time, the Algerian civil war was pitting that state against Islamists who had triumphed in electoral competition.) Frustrated by Ben Ali's refusal to deliver on his political promises to them, Islamists led demonstrations in the streets. These demonstrations were met with increasingly repressive measures (Hamdi 1998, 67–74). Isolated incidents of violence by the more militant wing of al-Nahda led to a military confrontation that resulted in the emasculation of the Islamist movement in 1991–92 (Murphy 1999, 193; Hamdi 1998).

This is a regime highly committed to social control. The shutdown of civil society is far out of proportion to the risk that Tunisia will face Algeria's difficulties, especially since Algeria itself has made some recent progress toward political liberalization. The Tunisian regime uses several strategies to prevent associational autonomy. First, no associations can exist without approval from the Ministry of the Interior. Permits to form associations are thus granted or withheld in light of regime interests (Bellin 1995). In addition to the legal constraints imposed by the Ministry of the Interior's visa system, the regime also controls associations financially; subsidies for associations are distributed on the basis of political subservience. RCD loyalists also attempt to infiltrate new associations or to duplicate them by forming ones of their own. Finally, the regime has not been reluctant to use force to contain civil society. Islamist activists in particular face harassment, arrest, and other repressive measures (Bellin 1995). These measures are also used against trade unionists, students, journalists, left-wing groups, and anyone else suspected of active opposition to the national consensus.[8]

Similarly, Tunisia's press under Ben Ali has become one of the most controlled in the Arab world. The French organization Reporters sans Frontières (RSF) calls press freedom in Tunisia nonexistent, stating that "news management is a fundamental building block of the police state in Tunisia." This international press organization provides a chilling view of Tunisia's present political climate: "All the institutions that could constitute countervailing powers to the regime—the judiciary, parliament, voluntary associations, political parties, universities, etc. have been systematically placed under government control" (RSF 1999).

In sum, the years of accelerated market liberalization in Tunisia have been associated with a sharp shift in the balance of class power toward urban and rural elites, while subordinate groups suffered sharp relative losses in economic and political resources. The democratization movement, which had been spearheaded by labor and mass mobilization, collapsed as the regime used corporatism and repression to reconfigure a once populist authoritarian order. An outlawed Islamist movement emerged as the primary opposition to a hegemonic state party intent on closing down all political space. These dynamics between masses and elites are mirrored in the neo-liberal transformation of the Tunisian countryside, which will be the subject of the next two chapters.

8. For details, see the Web site of Human Rights Watch, at <http://hrw.org/reports/world/tunisia-pubs.php>, under the heading "Overview of Human Rights Developments."

3

MARKETIZATION AND
THE RETRADITIONALIZATION
OF LOCAL POLITICS

The regime's ability to consolidate the emerging authoritarian system described in the last chapter may well depend on the state party's historical ability to maintain authoritarian controls in the countryside. Neo-liberal reforms in Tunisia have had a powerful impact on rural social structures and political organization, as they have on the national political economy. The severely flawed national elections in the 1980s and 1990s in Tunisia demonstrated that the RCD remains largely unchallenged in the countryside. Al-Nahda's electoral power was largely in urban areas, as was that of the small satellite parties.

This section begins a community study that will be completed in the next chapter. I attempt to demonstrate how traditional forms of social action in Tebourba, a large village in the fertile northwestern region of Tunisia (the Medjerda Valley region), were strengthened during the 1986–94 period of structural adjustment and rapidly changing property relations. Evidence presented here suggests that neo-liberal reforms in the agrarian parts of Tunisia have perpetuated patronage-based authoritarian control of the countryside. In order to co-opt equity concerns, the bureaucratic establishment and the wealthy promoted the revival of traditional mores of political and economic behavior, emphasizing a moral economy of reciprocal obligations. This meant reviving both traditional patronage and kinship networks and explicitly Islamic values and institutions. As the small peasantry adapted to the new environment through clientelism and other traditional village institutions, they became further alienated from formal political organizations. Thus, current state economic policies threaten the already scant ability of rural workers and poor peasants to participate effectively in national politics, associational life, and collective organizations.

In general, the literature on neo-liberal transformation and democratization focuses on the national level, and often considers the global context. A community study adds to this literature by providing a complementary, more concrete view of the political and social arrangements emerging from economic reform. The community study that follows suggests that the political and economic changes made by Ben Ali have rendered peasants more vulnerable to clientelism and control by the landed elites and the state bureaucracy. The numerous members of the small peasantry, those with insecure access to land and employment, are highly vulnerable to bureaucratic pressure. Parliamentary elections can be controlled by the délégués, or heads of the rural administrative districts, who are the only authorities able to dispense state patronage; opposition political candidates cannot do so. If other inducements are needed to produce desired results, the délégué can use the regime's security apparatus to intimidate the population. In this manner, local administrations, controlled by the minister of the interior in the highly centralized system, return a preponderance of parliamentary deputies friendly to the regime.

The case study is based on nine months of participant observation in Tebourba (1993–94), while a structural adjustment program was being implemented. Formal surveys of residents in different income groups, interviews with local and national government officials, and historical materials were also used. Finally, Mira Zussman's earlier work on the same community (1982) provided a helpful baseline with which to analyze the impact of market reforms on rural political and social life.

The overarching theme of the community study is how state elites deliberately stimulated cultural traditionalism in order to sustain neo-liberal reforms. The first section introduces Tebourba in the Tunisian context. The next section presents the contrasting theoretical interpretations of peasant behavior during increasing marketization. I take the position that the "rationality" of different peasant strategies, including individual profit maximization, depends to a significant degree on cultural systems, power relations, and structures of opportunities. The third section describes the historical power of the bureaucratic establishment and the landed gentry in rural communities in Tunisia, in order to establish their influential role in emerging social arrangements. The fourth section begins painting a portrait of cultural traditionalism by describing historical land tenure systems. Land privatization under structural adjustment gave rise to a multigenerational struggle over property rights between cultivators of the soil and various claimants from the upper strata of Tunisian society. The following sections fill out the discussion of traditional social organization by discussing kinship relationships, Islamic welfare mechanisms, and complex social arrangements relevant to the production and distribution of resources. The next chapter presents the full community study.

Economic Development in Tebourba

Tebourba is located in the fertile northwest agricultural region of Tunisia. Two mountain ranges, the Tellian Atlas and the Saharan Atlas, merge to form the Tunisian Dorsal, which runs from the southwest to the northeast of the country. The dorsal cuts off the Mediterranean region of northern Tunisia from the southern Tunisian steppe. Northern Tunisia enjoys the greatest amount of rainfall in the country, averaging more than four hundred millimeters a year. The Medjerda valley and plains, where Tebourba is located, lie between low wooded hills along the north coast and the area adjacent to the dorsal. Tunisia's largest river, the Medjerda, flowing from Algeria through the region, helped to make the area attractive for farmers. Traditionally the north has been known for extensive wheat fields; this part of "Ifriqia" was part of the granary of the Roman empire. Other rainfed crops, such as olives and dates, as well as animal husbandry, formed a part of traditional agriculture. Later crops included grapes, fruit, and vegetables.

To the south of the Dorsal, but still north of the Sahara desert, lies a steppe region receiving two to four hundred millimeters of rain annually. The summers can be very hot, and rainfed cultivation is more precarious than in the north. Land in this central region is often collectively held by tribes for animal grazing and some cultivation. However, along a narrow coastal strip called the Sahel, which runs from Sousse to Monastir and Mahidia, the presence of Mediterranean weather patterns has created a microclimate favorable to smallholders and settled village life (Amin 1970, 13). For centuries, this area has been known for the production and export of olive oil. Saharan agriculture is limited to alfa grass ranges and oasis agriculture. Stock tending becomes progressively more nomadic from north to south. Thus, roughly speaking, we can divide Tunisia into four regions: the north, central Tunisia, the Sahel, and the deep south of the Sahara.

There are many reasons to focus this study on northern Tunisia. Roughly two-thirds of the population is in the northern third of the country. The area north of the Dorsal, the Tell, is a valuable agricultural region, which has been at the center of the state's various modernization projects since independence. The rural community of Tebourba is located between the capital, Tunis, and the Algerian border. The nearness of central power weakened tribal structure.

Historically, city dwellers, frequently with ties to the (Ottoman) bey, influenced agricultural activities (Zghal 1980). Property rights have been ambiguous due to the conflicts between tenants and landlords. This was one of the earliest areas of French colonization and the center of the agricultural production cooperatives that defined Tunisian socialism.

At the outset, the purpose of the agricultural production cooperatives was to manage the lands newly freed from foreign ownership, and to do something about the high proportion of Tunisian peasants with small plots or insecure access to land and employment. Specifically, small holdings adjoining foreign estates were joined into single farming units of one to two thousand hectares (Simmons 1970, 39). Planners believed that cooperatives could apply the most modern technical solutions to problems of land development and absorb the unemployed.

The name "cooperatives" is deceptive, because the units were managed through a state hierarchy of organizations and technicians. It was decided at the start of the cooperative system to exclude Tunisian large landowners. They were deemed to be using modern techniques and diversified production patterns already. Authorities were also aware that the rural bourgeoisie would fiercely resist cooperativization, and the Socialist Destour still had close ties with this group. The small peasantry had less political power and less at stake with their microparcels, so they were merged, by force if necessary, into cooperatives.

Various factors contributed to the failure of the cooperative system. Peasants resented the top-down nature of the project. Local government authorities, responsible for maintaining local political stability, used the cooperatives to deal with unemployment instead of following the technical dictates of the agricultural engineers who spread through the countryside. In many instances the better private holdings of Tunisian large landowners had to be included. Some of the investments made during this period would not come to fruition until after the collapse of the movement. The Tunisian small property owners whose land was placed in a cooperative were promised a share of the cooperative's net benefits in proportion to how much land they put in and how much of their labor they contributed. However, very few property owners received benefits in return for their land in any of the cooperatives (Simmons 1970; Zamiti 1970).

After the collapse of the push for cooperatives, farmers in production cooperatives were given the option of leaving to farm their land as they had in the past. The law of September 9, 1969, on the reform of agricultural structures, which officially shifted policy toward increasing privatization, provided for land under cooperatives to be ceded to agricultural workers present on these lands, after returning the parcels that had been private lands to their original owners (FAO 1994, 23). Significantly, many of the smallholders who retrieved their land in 1969 eventually lost it to large landowners. They did not have the tools and animals needed to resume private production. Many resorted to borrowing from wealthier farmers, became indebted, and lost their farms (Zamiti 1970, 52–53).

In practice only about fifty cooperatives were distributed to landless laborers and agricultural technicians. The rest of the agricultural production cooperatives on the largest and best land, around two hundred of them, continued to be cultivated by cooperative workers, and no steps were taken to cede ownership to them (Zamiti 1970). From 1970 until the early 1980s, land privatization policy "began with the return of private lands to their owners and the cession of a part of the state lands to members of the private sector: older activists of the nationalist movement, young farmers, agricultural technicians and occupants of good faith" (Gharbi 1998, 86). However, the end result of this policy was the distribution of a small amount of land to stabilize the small peasantry, while the lion's share of the land ended up in the hands of large farmers who had already owned more than fifty hectares and who were also provided with the exclusive benefit of state-subsidized credit (Radwan, Jamal, and Ghose 1991, 40–41).

Until 1982, the remaining agricultural workers on cooperatives continued to expect a parcel of their own. During this period little investment was made in cooperatives. On August 6, 1982, a new code of agricultural investment was promulgated. The code created the Land Improvement Companies (Sociétés de Mise en Valeur et de Développement Agricole, SMVDA). This was a new form of management, intended to correct for earlier poor management and underinvestment on valuable agricultural land (FAO 1994, 23). Private investors were entrusted with the management of entire cooperatives, supported by public credit and with technological assistance, along with long-term lease rates far below market prices.

During the period 1982–90, the program developed slowly, with only twenty-six land improvement companies created. However, the state planned to restructure all of the cooperatives in this manner eventually, prior to outright privatization.[1] After a national consultation in 1990, the pace of privatization increased, with the support of two World Bank agricultural sector loans. The

1. Director of the Ministry of State Lands, interviewed by the author.

community study of Tebourba that follows examines how rural social and political organization adapted to this period of state-led economic liberalization.

Increasing Marketization and Peasant Communities

The debates between those who view peasant communities as moral economies and those who conceive of peasants as rational actors are well known. Since my central argument, that a Tunisian moral economy was reinforced, is situated in this debate, it may be useful to present the contrasting interpretations of peasant behavior during increasing marketization. Moral economy approaches usually explain human social action by focusing on community or village-level norms of behavior. The central argument is that pre-capitalist agricultural villages develop elaborate forms of social exchange, which operate to redistribute some resources and provide all community members with subsistence. Reciprocity and limited redistribution are the central tenets of this social order. Other mechanisms of community welfare and insurance include diffuse patron-client ties, redistributive gift-giving, and village-level provision of resources for the destitute. Individuals who are raised in these communities usually follow the rules of these traditional institutions (Polanyi 1957; Scott 1976; Wolf 1969).

Some moral economists acknowledge that increasing marketization may partially dissolve patrimonial relations between landowning employers and attached workers (Scott 1985, 182–83). Others argue that while agrarian capitalism may weaken traditional bonds and mutual obligations, in many cases the system of patron-client ties is restored. Often, "profit-oriented cash crop farmers in search of reliable, committed labor have established neo-patrimonial relations with their employees through gifts, accessible credit, job security, and other welfare arrangements" (Rudolph and Rudolph 1987, 371). Those who suffer relative losses during capitalist transformation continue to press rich villagers and landlords to maintain a sense of community and obligation to the poor (Scott 1985). In general, in spite of changes spurred by the penetration of markets, the physical mobility of village residents, and state institutions that serve as a partial safety net, moral economists attribute some continued importance to community welfare and insurance mechanisms, even as different forms of peasant behavior evolve over time.

By contrast, in a rational actor approach to peasant communities, Samuel Popkin (1979) vigorously attacks the claim that pre-capitalist peasant societies provided household social insurance against the risks of agriculture. The village-level insurance and welfare mechanisms failed miserably, due to collective action problems. Insurance and welfare are public goods. A public good is defined as any good such that those who do not pay for it cannot be excluded from sharing in its consumption (Olsen 1971, 14–15). Collective action theorists generally doubt that communities can organize to provide public goods without the use of sanctions and incentives that imply an outside force. In particular, these theorists cite the tendency of people to free-ride, that is, to enjoy the good without contributing to its provision.

According to Popkin, the inadequacy of community insurance and welfare mechanisms led peasants to use investment logic in deciding to what extent to participate in these mechanisms. In this view, community norms of redistribution and extensive reciprocity were not widely followed. The family maximizes utility by applying cost-benefit logic to political and economic decision making. Investment in future personal welfare supersedes village norms and procedures, which are characterized by reciprocity and welfare insurance. This rational actor approach suggests that the poor, middle peasants, and the wealthy are willing and able to ignore traditional obligations and exploit the opportunities of increasing marketization.

My stance on these issues is that of a cultural materialist. From the long-term economic point of view, everyone is risk-averse and also restrained by their social systems, relationships, and settings—the real question is the context defining the nature of the risk, the probabilities of success. Change the nature of the risk and changes in behavior will follow. Individual profit maximization is "rational" if the individual has the skills and opportunities to take advantage. Given opportunities for success, cultivators will become profit maximizers, although what is profit, what is valued, may be culturally defined.[2]

Ultimately, the opposite has happened during state-led economic liberalization in Tebourba: for most peasants the new market arrangements have increased risk but not opportunity. Market reforms have threatened, and even catastrophically affected, some people's subsistence. In this context, complex social arrangements anchored in blood ties, reciprocity, and redistribution become more vital to many community members. In other words, constraints on individual behavior in the form of cultural systems, historical relationships, relative power, opportunity structures, and environmental settings must be

2. Although John Waterbury may not agree with these assertions, comments by him influenced the position I take here.

part of an analysis of peasant behavior during increasing marketization, although the analysis must not lose sight of actor autonomy altogether.

The general thrust of this perspective on peasant behavior is shared by several scholars. Anne Swidler (1986) breaks down culture into components that provide the tools of habits, skills, and styles, from which people construct strategies of social action. Strategies of action require skills, which various members of the community will possess to varying degrees. The term "strategy" refers to a general way of organizing action: depending upon a network of kin and friends, for example, or relying on one's skills in the market. Even when goals change, actors' strategies of action may persist.

Robert Axelrod (1986), in explaining emerging strategies of social action, asserts that deductions based on the theory that people are fully rational actors making detailed calculations about the future are less empirically sound than those that assume that people choose their strategies by trial and error. Effective strategies are more likely to be retained than ineffective ones. Community norms offer types of strategies for actors to consider. He has defined norms: "A norm exists in a given social setting to the extent that individuals usually act in a certain way and are often punished when seen not to be acting in this way" (Axelrod 1986, 1097). Axelrod's trial-and-error approach allows the introduction of new strategies as occasional mutations of old strategies.

Edward Hedican (1986) argues that an individualistic actor-oriented perspective on social organization is not apt to yield new information on the relationship between decisions and wider social relationships, and between decisions and available resources. Hedican is right to point out that a person's decisions cannot be divorced from decisions made by others with whom that person interacts, and that a person's interests and decisions are often modified by more powerful people.

In sum, rural actors can potentially use a number of strategies to organize action and obtain resources, including those that aim at maximizing individual profit, thus presumably fitting the culture of the market. However, in what follows, I will make the case that neo-liberal reforms and the political strategies Tunisian state agents have pursued at the local level combine to promote traditional patronage and kinship networks and Islamic values and institutions. The emerging neo-traditional social arrangements are based on the strengthening of rural notables, the accommodation of the rural poor to the revived order through clientelism, and a greater reliance by political elites on Islamic welfare mechanisms to maintain social order. Thus, in Tebourba, and likely elsewhere in Tunisia during the current marketization phase, structural opportunities for employment and the modification of strategies by elites combine to limit the range of viable strategies for subordinate groups.

The previous chapter described a range of structural adjustment policies that benefited the rural gentry. However, it is the privatization of land belonging to the state-managed agricultural cooperatives, in particular, that represents the greatest setback to the small peasantry and pushes them most toward traditional peasant institutions. The historical summary which follows will aid in understanding the context in which land tenure problems originated; it seeks to clarify the balance of political power influencing state policy, and to deepen our understanding of the link between market-oriented reforms and the evolution of political and social organization. A historical perspective, in short, will help us fully appreciate how recent market-oriented reforms have affected a multigenerational struggle for economic and political resources among different groups in the countryside.

Rural Administration and the Historical Balance of Political Power

The framework of Tunisia's current rural political structure was established in the nineteenth century under Ottoman rulers. From 1569 until 1881 Tunisia was nominally part of the Ottoman Empire. The bey of Tunis became virtually independent of the Ottoman Empire in 1705, and the office became hereditary.[3] Distinguished families in the various regions provided services and support to the bey, often in exchange for semi-feudal rights over land and tax collection. These relationships provided a basis for rudimentary representative institutions.

From 1705 the bey had a number of *quwwad* (regional representatives of the state, singular *qāʾid*) stationed in the major towns, from which rural affairs were managed through tribal delegates or *shuykh* (singular *shaykh*). The quwwad headed *qāʾidat* (singular *qāʾida*), which were divided into *mashayikh* (singular *mashyakha*) headed by the various shuykh. Initially, the quwwad were elected by the tribe or tribal clans they governed. This electoral system, to a degree, continued into the French Protectorate (1881–1956). However, for various reasons, including the complexity of the Protectorate's bureaucracy,

3. For a detailed discussion of Tunisian administrative structures see Ashford 1967, 60–93.

tribal patterns began to disappear and regional notables began to select the quwwad.

In addition to the qaʾidat and mashayikh in rural areas, municipal councils were developed in large towns. In 1858, Muhammad Bey established a municipal council for the capital, Tunis. This council was dominated by the most powerful families of the time. Other densely populated areas were granted councils soon after. Thus, under the beylical system, local administration comprised both municipal councils in urban areas and quwwad to supervise rural communities. The village shaykh served as another link between the village and the national government.

The French retained the basic structure of the government intact, while placing French overseers over the indigenous officials. One important change on the village level was that the shaykh was now ultimately responsible to and often appointed by the French. These local "leaders" still reported to the quwwad. By the turn of the century many shuykh were chosen on criteria other than ethnicity or tribal groupings. In 1905 territorial units were established by the French, for which the qaʾid would make a list of qualified native candidates for shaykh positions. By 1925, the local officials were appointed by the central authorities of the Protectorate without the aid of qaʾid nominations (Ashford 1967, 68).

Tunisia's single-party system, installed after independence in 1956, built on this foundation of local political organization. The Neo-Destour created an organization parallel to that of the state and developed an effective nationwide system of social control. From the outset, the party used the qaʾidat, mashayikh, and municipal system as a base for its own rural administration. One or more party cells were assigned to each mashyakha to mobilize support for the national movement and the party (Moore 1965, 78).

The post-independence provincial system, still in operation today, is headed by the Ministry of the Interior. Tunisia is divided into twenty-three states, each under the supervision of a governor. The governors are granted undisputed control of the police and all government services in their territory, and generally meet once a month with the president himself. Initially the governors were handpicked by the president and their powers were not legally defined (Ashford 1967, 74). Governors head states, which are divided into delegations. Each of these delegations is headed by a délégué, who reports to the governor.

Until the mid-1970s, the délégués were assisted by local shuykh in various sectors of the community. In 1975, the role of shaykh became purely administrative and the title was changed to ͨumda. These new figures can be appointed by the Ministry of the Interior and may not have local ties.

The use of the Ministry of the Interior officials to control the countryside in Tunisia is similar to the situation in Morocco. In Morocco, the Ministry of the Interior "stands out from all others as an instrument of monarchical control," (Waterbury 1970, 280). As in Morocco, the council system has been used as a foil while local power remains in the administrative posts of the ministry. In fact, according to Douglas Ashford, the Tunisian Municipal Law of 1957 imposed much more stringent restrictions on the councils than the similar legislation of Morocco (Ashford 1967, 81).

Local government in the form of the elected municipal councils is subordinated to the authority of the Ministry of the Interior officials. It has been pointed out that governors viewed the councils as contributing to the harmony of the regime: "the governor hoped that the new council would consecrate itself to the community's urban, aesthetic and general well-being, and thereby contribute to concord and national unity" (Ashford 1967, 80). Official restrictions on the councils include a prohibition on expressing political views, and all matters discussed at meetings have to be cleared by Tunis. The councils involve themselves in matters such as road improvements, drainage, electrification, and public transport. These and other areas of municipal management also generally have to be approved by superior authority in Tunis (Ashford 1967, 81; King 1997). In addition, the dominant party's development projects, frequently initiated at election time, take precedence over council efforts.

The majority of Tunisians are represented de facto by their governor, and their local needs and desires have to be communicated through the délégué, to the governor, and finally to the Minister of the Interior (Ashford 1967, 81–82). In sum, the bureaucratic establishment, by allying itself with socioeconomic elites, has come to dominate rural areas in Tunisia politically, economically, and socially. Much of the story of the politics of adjustment in rural Tunisia begins with an analysis of the role of the dominant party and local officials in the Ministry of Interior. An understanding of rural social organization will help to further clarify this role.

Traditional Social Organization and the Land Tenure System

In an agrarian context social organization, whether composed of complex social exchanges or primarily individualistic, is related to the land tenure system. "Land tenure" refers to the division of a bundle of property rights and duties, both customary and legal, among the state, individual families, tribes, and other relevant social forms. These include use rights, crop sharing, grazing, leasing, inheritance, and borrowing (El-Ghonemy 1990). Through their land policies, neo-liberal reforms cut through both land tenure and social arrangements that over time have evolved to provide a range of more or less effective strategies for rural dwellers to obtain resources.

Today, rigorous written laws attempt to demarcate land ownership in Tunisia, whereas in the past, under the beylical system, peasants' relationships to their plots were very supple. Communitarian traditions were assimilated, to a degree, into judicial categories. "Collective land" referred to the projection of the rights of groups, not individuals. These were lands of independent tribes, found especially in the southern and central portions of the country. In these regions, the lack of rainfall made planting crops a very risky affair. Transhumance dominated animal husbandry and the land was used more often as a travel route and pasture than as acreage for cultivation. The validity of property rights over collective land depended in reality on a relation of force and custom among tribes (raids and counter-raids could lead to different groups monopolizing the land) and between tribes and the beylical regime (Valensi 1985).

Private property, *melk* in Arabic, most central to the spirit of capitalism, was only predominant in the regions with strong sedentary occupations and around some villages, in a small part of agricultural space (Zghal 1980, 11–30). True melk land was found in regions with the best soil and water, and was regularly cultivated. Most of it was included in the olive-growing region of the Sahel. A mass of smallholders prevented significant conflict between large landowners and peasants without land.

Melk land formed a small part of the northern cereal region of the Tell, where our case study, Tebourba, is located and where the agricultural cooperative movement was centered. This area was known for melk cereal lands (Poncet 1962). The cereal lands were more extensive and expansive than true melk lands. Titles of land were less precise for these large holdings. These holdings, called *henchirs,* were at least several dozen hectares, and averaged several hundred. Pastoral nomadism was more prevalent, in addition to intensive dense sedentary life. In this zone between the capital, Tunis, and Algeria, tribal structure was weakened by the nearness of central power and the military agents in the military centers of Béja and Kef (Zghal 1980). City dwellers, frequently with ties to the bey, influenced agricultural activities.

Fiefdoms, concessions (*iqtaʿ*) granted by the bey to a political figure or tribe, were often created and expanded in the north in the period. But property rights in iqta^c were precarious and revocable. The beneficiary did not have the right, nor was it in his interest, to expel peasants installed on land transformed into iqta^c. Peasants paid tribute in crops to their feudal lords.

Religious custom provided the bey with other means to impinge on the property rights of tribal groups. Land that was not regularly cultivated was referred to as "dead." The bey, as head of the Muslim community, always possessed the right to grant land considered dead that escaped private property status under written land tenure laws. In other instances, Muslim traditions authorized the use of dead lands by any Muslim.

Sometimes rural notables turned dead lands into their own rental property. Historically, land was plentiful in Tunisia. The problem was the lack of men and women to work it. Wealth was not measured in space owned but in planted land, trees, harnesses, and livestock. The real cleavage was between those who possessed farm equipment and those who did not (Zghal 1980). Small agriculturalists of the north, as parts of a weakened tribal structure, also often lost land privileges when they lacked work tools. This occurred mainly to those who had suffered a series of bad years due to drought, excessive taxation or feudalism, or theft and violence. Notables sometimes helped these "tool-less" peasants to once again obtain the means to cultivate land. In exchange the peasants began to pay rent on the land (Poncet 1962, 68).

In addition to collective land, melk, and iqta^c, Muslim tradition had another way to appropriate the soil: *habous,* endowments of land. Habous was divided into private and public usage. Income derived from public habous was given over to the support of some public cause, such as a school, mosque, or hospital. Any land committed to a private habous was designated to support the heirs of the owner, so long as the family line might continue. However, should the line of descent cease, the private habous would become public habous. No one could confiscate habous land. The beneficiary could be changed, but not the state of the land itself. It was, for the most part, safe even against capricious confiscation by the bey and others. Habous also could not be taxed. These benefits led many private landowners to obtain habous titles. In 1881 about 25 percent of Tunisian land, a large portion of the richest and including much of the fertile Medjerda valley (where the case study is located), reposed in habous (Ling 1967, 62).

Public habous also threatened the tribes of northern Tunisia. According to Abdelkader Zghal (1980), the beys, in order to legitimize their power, often transformed vast domains exploited by peasant communities into habous dedicated to a maraboutic lineage (tribes with religious functions, believed to be descendants of the Prophet) or a pious project. In these cases, the bey received a portion of the revenue in the form of taxes and fees.

In sum, in northern Tunisia property rights were contested by various elites and peasant cultivating communities. In other areas powerful tribes dominated less fertile land. However, in the north, the property rights of populations living "with their crop lands, cemeteries, silos, marabouts, and sometimes trees and private gardens [were opposed to] the pretensions of the feudals, chiefs of tribes, war factions, caids, beneficiaries of a beylical domain, and the beys" (Poncet 1962, 54).

In spite of the powerful forces that weakened their tribal structure, peasants in the north did not cultivate as individuals. Efforts were made to maintain kinship solidarity. According to Jean Poncet, "cereal regions are rarely regions of owned property. They are usually collectives or fiefdoms. The laborer is never alone. He is part of a group, douar [group of houses], fraction of a tribe, a family that aids him in his work and shares rights of ownership" (Poncet 1962, 52). In these cereal regions, even when powerful figures possessed titles to henchirs of hundreds of hectares or more, frequently the titles were challenged by the cultivators of the land with hereditary claims to it.

Still, some cultivators fell on the hardest of times, especially the landless and tool-less with the weakest kinship links. These were the main candidates for the various sharecropping arrangements, of which *khammas* contracts were the most common in the cereal lands of the north. The khammas peasant is paid one-fifth of the harvest for supplying the labor power necessary for an agricultural campaign. In principle the "landowner" provided the other four-fifths necessary for production: tools, plow animals, seeds, and land.

In the northern region, which later formed the core of the lands put into cooperatives, in the 1900s (just prior to French colonization) most of the land was held in iqta^c by regime dignitaries and in public habous. Ancient real possessors of the soil cultivated the land while being subjugated by a class of notables (Zghal 1980; Poncet 1962). These peasants frequently lived in tent villages while growing cereals, raising livestock, and tending to olive trees, sometimes under sharecropping arrangements like the *khammesat* system.

In the mid-1880s a subsistence economy predominated. Tunisia was sparsely populated. The land tenure regime, fashioned over the course of centuries of insecurity, found its expression in law and Koranic customs. Land was usually immobilized. Property rights were shared between powerful figures in the beylical regime, tribes, or pious foundations and cultivators who occupied the land and passed their property rights down from generation to generation.

Social Relations: A Tribal Society

A portrait of traditional rural social action and the historical and cultural context in which social relations have been formed, together with the land tenure arrangements already described, will provide a frame of reference for the range of strategies available to Tunisian peasants. Until around the middle of the nineteenth century, Tunisia was a segmentary tribal society dominated by urban and tribal elites (Valensi 1985; Montagne 1931; Zghal 1980).

In a segmentary system, the individual and the nuclear family are part of a group. The extended family is likely the smallest unit capable of separating from the community. In nineteenth-century Tunisia those with weakened tribal ties were the most vulnerable to exploitative relationships. Communal land ownership and patron-client ties between "landowners" and hereditary occupant-cultivators increased the importance of complex social relations.

The exchange of goods was also an important part of social relations. Alongside subsistence agriculture in pre-Protectorate Tunisia, market exchanges existed both within tribes and among them. Tunisian markets, *suqs,* were well known for the expert calculations and business acumen of their merchants as well as internal and external trade in products such as the red fez, or *chechia.* Still, the predominance of subsistence agriculture insured the prominence of complex social exchange. Production and consumption usually occurred at a level above the nuclear family (Poncet 1962; Zghal 1980; Valensi 1985).

Social relations, especially kinship ties, have been paramount in Tunisian peasant traditions. As Valensi phrased it, "The individual is immediately placed in a group—the descendants of X . . . which in turn is placed in a larger group. The individual is thus at the center of a series of concentric circles of which the last, the largest, is the tribe. In this way, the individual does not exist by himself; he is inseparable from the community. In the same way, the nuclear family has no status; . . . [the] initial stage is [the] extended family" (Valensi 1985, 25).

In a segmentary society, the social hierarchy of individuals and groups is dependent on extra-economic norms such as religion and kinship ties. Each large tribal unit is formed by a certain number of groups fitting together. The first level is that of the entire tribe, the second is the large tribal sections, the third the principal lineages, and so on to the family unit. In Tunisia, political organization operated according to a formula of opposition and solidarity. Rivalry occurred among units at the same level of organization, e.g., lineage vs.

lineage. Rural lineages then combined to face a similar cluster of lineages, which in turn might combine to face a rival tribe.

In this type of social organization absolute authority did not rest with a lone shaykh or tribe. Authority was distributed at each level in the tribal structure. The exercise of political power was limited to specific situations in which a tribe or section acted as a group. Kinship created occasions for strife over such things as water holes and grazing lands. There were raids and counter-raids. Violence was a collective affair; within a tribe, different offshoots of a branch might fight one another. At times, hereditary conflicts could develop between tribes, perhaps due to the infrequency of intermarriage or to armed conflict. Over time, patterns of alliances developed, with various tribes repeatedly banding together during periods of conflict. These alliances were known as *soffs*. Maraboutic tribes and the marabouts, or local saints, frequently helped resolve both minor and major conflicts.

In Tunisia under the beys, tribes managed their own internal affairs. The central power had the military force to govern but possessed limited administrative capacity. All the tribes were subjects of the bey, and their allegiance was expressed first and foremost by the payment of taxes. Loyal tribal groups, shuykh, and government officials or quwwad were all used to collect taxes. The bey owed the people national defense and the provision of justice. Tribes tried various ways to avoid taxation. The bey and his agents had to evaluate how much taxation they could impose on peasants without inducing them to leave the land for a nomadic life.

A tax revolt in 1864 is often cited to portray the dynamics of rural political organization in nineteenth-century Tunisia (Valensi 1985; Chater 1978; Slama 1970). This was a tremendous uprising against the state. The two principal taxes on agriculture were the ʿushur, on cereal harvests, and the *qanun*, on olives. A head tax, the *mejba,* had been instituted in 1856, and was especially controversial. Every adult male was obliged to pay. No community was exempted, and the poor paid as much as the rich. It was a heavy and humiliating tax, the culmination of the progressive rise in taxation on all rural activity. Although historical evidence suggests the mejba was not the first head tax levied in Tunisia, people objected to it on the grounds that Muslims are not liable to a head tax, according to Islam (Valensi 1985, 231).

As Tunisia was opening up to European commerce in the first half of the nineteenth century, the peasantry were overexploited by rising taxes. The beylical state fell into severe debt as the aristocracy increased their consumption of luxuries; the cost of armaments to deal with European power raised public debt as well, and there was increasing competition from European manufacturers (Mahjoub 1987). The beylical state increased taxes and shook up traditional political and social relations to deal with the changing economic conditions.

In 1864, the mejba was doubled and the tribes launched a near-general revolt against the power of the quwwad, the symbols of oppression. They demanded that taxes be reduced and the ʿushur and qanun be eliminated. For a few months nearly all tribes, rich and poor alike, challenged the state. Although some of the wealthy may have been trying to protect their property, some were active participants in the movement, along with other notables, such as religious groups and jurists (Valensi 1985, 239–40).

However, after a time, some tribes allied themselves with the bey to subjugate the others. The tribes who did so were the same ones who had sided with his dynastic line in a violent struggle over power over one hundred years earlier. The opposing tribes were invariably the ones who had sided with the dynasty's challengers. The example demonstrates the power of a soff and segmentary dynamics in explaining traditional political organization. The agents of the bey used the power of traditional alliances and hereditary conflicts to end the greatest internal challenge the beylical state had ever faced. However, at other times the beylical state was able to siphon off resources from agricultural production and leave the hinterlands to their normal rhythms of life.

In sum, land tenure has long been central to Tunisian rural social organization. Tribal alliances have also demonstrated a long-standing durability. The 1864 revolt foreshadowed dynamics that would appear in changed form in the 1980s and 1990s. The state ended a populist era and recommitted itself to a social system dependent on an alliance between urban and rural elites. The long struggle over property rights between rural notables in the beylical regime and cultivators of the soil would be ultimately decided by the state when it turned over cooperative land to the descendants of the state's powerful allies in the countryside. These landed elites would provide the regime with its most potent source of support.

Islam and the Networks of Life

There is another important aspect of rural social organization in Muslim parts of the world. Within peasant communities, traditionally life unfolded according to the rhythms of Islam. *Maʿunah* (mutual aid), reciprocal exchanges during Islamic celebrations or for strictly economic reasons, characterized the internal workings of each community's social system. Various authors have noted a system of obligatory gift-giving through public festivals linked to sacred rites of Islam (Maunier 1927, 11–97; Poncet 1962; Association Française 1896). These forms of exchange frequently involved some redistribution of wealth from rich to poor. Ostentatious gift-giving provided the donor with prestige and power and the recipient with resources. Wealth was frequently dissipated in this manner. The exchanges mixed material interests, mutual aid, political advantage, and religious imperatives.

Islamic welfare mechanisms played a central part in the regulated exchange of goods outside of the market. Religious holidays were, and to an extent continue to be, times of public festivals and occasions to redistribute wealth through aid to the poor. Al-Eid al-Kabir commemorates the sacrifice of Abraham. On this holiday, it was customary to sacrifice an animal and distribute part of the meat to the needy. Al-Mawled al-Nabiyy, the holiday celebrating the birth of the Prophet, was a feast day. Each day of Ramadan, the month of fasting, ended with opulent meals and the religious obligation to aid the poor, and the tenth day of the month, the *ashurah*, was a special feast day. The holiday celebrating the end of Ramadan, al-Eid as-Saghir, called for communal feasts. The zakat, the Muslim tithe, frequently occurred at harvest time, when the poorest residents received some aid from wealthier peasants. These customs are described by an early colonial observer:

> [First there is] the Zakat; all good Muslims once a year must take two and a half per hundred from their fortune to distribute to the poor. On al-Eid as-Saghir, the day after Ramadan, each Muslim must give to the poor a certain quantity of the most abundant food crop in the country. Three liters for each member of the family. For the purification of the young, Zahat-al-fitr, the kaffara [expiation] consists of distributing sixty loaves of bread to the poor, or of freeing a slave. Giving alms to the poor is recommended as a daily practice, but occurs particularly on the nights of religious festivals. Giving alms is the best way to attain divine favor. (Association Française 1896, 485)

In addition to the ritual exchanges defined by the Islamic calendar, public displays of exchange and redistribution occurred at the time of important events in the life of the family: births, marriages, circumcisions, and funerals. Normally, these gifts were publicized, either by displaying them with their donors or verbally, sometimes in a ceremonial announcement by someone akin to a town crier (Maunier 1927, 60). These "archaic" forms of exchange, the remnants of which are evident in our own customs of exchanging gifts and invitations, have been especially widespread in North Africa (Maunier 1927).

Hospitality between tribes and families was also part of systematic exchange. This was considered an obligation and a right. The head of a tribe or village was especially obligated to be generous. Frequent distributions of gifts maintained status, respect, and power. Authority required ostentation, and consumption and donations to others were symbols of greatness (Maunier 1927, 485). Thus, generally speaking, local values encouraged rich men, looking for prestige, to reinvest their money through religious payments, which typically implied redistribution. This partially offset the taking of peasant resources by the wealthy through the sharecropping system and other methods (Hopkins 1983, 59).

Reciprocal exchanges occurred also in family and village labor. "The men ploughed, harvested, and threshed, gathered olives, sheared sheep, and constructed houses; the women prepared the reserves of food and set up the looms—all of which activities were publicly announced and collectively undertaken at the home of the man or woman who invited the relatives and workers. It was the obligation of the host family to feed the co-workers and to reciprocate the same service when the occasion arose" (Valensi 1985, 175). Masons and others with technical skills collaborated on construction projects, but as part of the social affair, not as contractors. Family and friends led the execution of the project. Complex mutual assistance served to strengthen community relations. Whoever exempted him- or herself from these norms risked being excluded from the social fabric and the circulation of much of the community's goods and services.

Patron-client ties formed another part of pre-Protectorate social structure. Patron-client or clientele relations rest on an exchange of goods and services between individuals of unequal social and economic status (Anderson 1986, 25). In areas where notables received tribute from hereditary occupants of the land, personal relationships developed that implied mutual obligations. Peasants surrendered part of their production to their patrons, whom they expected to provide aid during emergencies, participate in the limited redistributive networks described above, and use their influence with the state in matters of importance. Needing the peasants' labor to cultivate the land, to which the peasants had customary access anyway, the notables had reason to maintain some reciprocity in their unequal relationship. Thus, clientele relations existed in addition to the more dominant kinship organization of the segmentary system. Clientelism could also develop between weaker and stronger members of the same lineage group or tribe.

The sum total of the complex social relations described here means that a moral economy prevailed in pre-Protectorate rural Tunisia. The individual pursuit of material gain occurred in a web of social relations. Reference to these social relations is clearly more important to understanding rural social organization at that time than is focusing primarily on rational individual maximizing strategies. The extended family was normally the smallest unit in the production and consumption of resources. The subsistence economy was more important than the market economy. Reciprocity and redistribution through ritual exchanges, often as part of the religious imperatives of Islam, limited the individual pursuit of material goods. Many of these dynamics would appear again in a changed form in the 1980s and 1990s, when state agents manipulated cultural traditionalism in order to reduce political tensions caused by the implementation of grossly inequitable structural adjustment policies in the countryside. However, before more contemporary changes in social organization are discussed, the next section will examine changes in land tenure and social forms during the colonial era. The colonial period is an essential part of the multigenerational struggle over property rights between cultivator-occupiers of the land and rural notables connected to the beylical regime, a struggle finally resolved by the neo-liberal transformation of the current Tunisian government.

The Colonial Period: 1881–1956

At the onset of colonization in 1881, the population of Tunisia was estimated to be 900,000. Two thousand people lived in the qaᶜida of Tebourba (Poncet 1962, 44–45). Epidemics and famines in 1867–69 had likely cut the population in half. Life depended primarily on the production of grains, olive oil, and livestock. Jean Poncet estimated that 120,000 families living by agriculture produced two million quintals of grain in the 1880s, 100,000 hectoliters of oil, and around four million head of livestock. The average consumption value of these products was estimated in 1951 at around four hundred francs a year per family. Significantly, the purchasing power of the average Tunisian family income in the 1880s was three times what it was around 1948 (Poncet 1962, 135).

In Tebourba, there were 36,470 hectares of land. Cereals covered 16,850 hectares. There were 105 henchirs, with an average size of 300 hectares, comprising 185 *douars,* or tent villages. Mud houses or *gourbis,* habitations inferior to tents, were also widespread in Tebourba, indicating the presence of poor khammas and cereal lands owned communally by fracturing tribes, lineages, extended

families, and groups of semi-sedentary laborers giving tribute to absentee owners: in total there were 1600 gourbis, 300–400 tents, and 400 houses in Tebourba
and the outlying areas (Poncet 1962, 53, 118).

Colonialism encouraged large landholdings and a decline in peasant standards of living in Tunisia. The technological changes and improved production
techniques involved in the creation of a "modern" agricultural sector did not
represent gains for the majority of the peasantry. In general, landlord power
was reinforced against various occupant-cultivators, a pattern already apparent
in the decades prior to colonization.

In this regard, the commercialization of grain led to systematic efforts to
tie khammas workers to their patrons in order to produce more grain for
the Mediterranean market. In 1874 Prime Minister Khayr al-Din codified the
khammesat. The khammas could abandon his estate only if he became an independent farmer working on his own account. If he lacked the tools and other
resources to make it on his own, the qaʾid was obliged to renew his contract
with the farmer. Bodily force could be used against all khamamisa not fulfilling
their obligations.

The various forms of feudal tenure that gave both peasants and landlords
certain rights to a given area, without either being considered the absolute
owner, gradually gave way to modern private property in the colonial era. The
rights of peasants and nomadic herders began to be abrogated, as the wealthy
used their superior power to assert absolute property rights on the Western
model. The land transfers involved primarily the French, but also a significant
number of Tunisian notables.

Increasing demands by landlords, made more powerful by changing land
policy, and a growing government preference for cash taxes meant that more
money was loaned to peasants. This became another route to land loss, as their
property was used to secure loans. They often had to borrow in order to buy
food or implements, and inability to pay often meant loss of land.

During the Protectorate there was more investment in favored agricultural
areas, and they were more thoroughly exploited than had been traditional in
Tunisia. Foreign demand for new crops, such as wine grapes and fruits, as well
as the growing French market for Tunisian wheat, provided new incentives for
producers. However, the growth of a profitable Western market for agricultural
goods tended to increase European and Tunisian landlord income and power.
Peasants were probably more widely exploited than was traditional.

Certainly some Tunisian groups benefited from increasing marketization
during the Protectorate. Among these were the landlords, who strengthened

their hold on the land, and those peasants who owned land producing goods for export. Middlemen such as moneylenders, traders, and merchants had new opportunities for profit, and could turn their gains into land ownership. Owners of tools could rent them. However, the growth of a market economy allowed these groups to enrich themselves at the expense of the peasant majority. The main outline of the trends during the Protectorate, which worsened peasant conditions while bringing about modernization, will be covered in the following sections.

The Development of Modern Private Property

In 1881, at the start of the French Protectorate, only limited acreage was available for French investment: principally two large tracts known as Sidi Tabet and Enfida, owned by the Société Marseillaise. The expansion of French ownership came at the expense of Tunisian owners and by some modification of religious laws (Harber 1973, 309).

The legal concept of land ownership was changed in 1885. The Land Registration Act, patterned on the Torrens Land Act of Australia, was intended to simplify land transactions. It permitted all landowners to register their property with the specially devised *tribunal mixte,* an institution consisting of three French and three Tunisian judges with French executive oversight. Titles were granted to Tunisians by Tunisian judges after a period during which claims were published and could be challenged. All other business took place before French judges unless a dispute involved Tunisians, in which event two Tunisian and two French judges ruled on the case. In effect, this process wiped the ownership rolls clean and started them over again. Land registration was removed from the Islamic courts, called *shariᶜa,* from that moment on.

All unregistered property remained under the jurisdiction of the shariᶜa courts, and there was no requirement that land be registered. In 1888 the bey instituted a law directed against underutilized habous land. *Enzel* rights provided for the use of land in public habous, by permitting the land to be leased or by allowing a party to use the property in ways rivaling private ownership. In 1888 an act permitted putting enzel land up for auction. The highest bidder obtained the privilege of renting the land. In 1903 applications were granted for enzel rights on cultivated land. By 1908, 108,000 acres had been accorded to Europeans by these means, and 38,000 to Tunisians (Harber 1973, 311).

In 1898 another decree was issued, legitimizing the exchange of land placed in habous for money or other land. If money was exchanged, the money had to be used to put new property in habous. The land exchanged for that in habous took on its restrictions (Harber 1973, 312), while the old habous property could be treated as private property. This process meant that the best habous land could be taken over by new landlords while the inferior land went into habous. Wealth in money or land was needed to make these transactions. Peasant cultivators stood to lose access and property rights to Tunisia's better agricultural lands held in habous.

Beylical domains, those held in iqta^c by feudal elements, and forest lands also attracted the attention of the French. In 1890 forest lands were demarcated and sold to the French. People who had possessed titles to these lands could be expelled from them. Beylical "private state" domains, largely those of the bey, were reclassified as "private" domains and made available at a nominal price of ten francs per hectare. At the time, agricultural land in France cost two thousand francs per hectare. In 1881 there were 400,000 hectares in private state domains. Tunisians claimed 33,000 hectares of this land. By 1938 1,000,000 hectares of forest lands and private domains had been made available for private ownership, with the intention of facilitating French settlement while permitting Tunisian ownership. The negative result, from a Tunisian standpoint, was that a large number of people were evicted from the land, and drifted to the towns or became migrant laborers (Ziadeh 1969, 41).

Land policy under the Protectorate, in addition to bolstering French land ownership and Tunisian landlord rights in various ways, helped to create a dual agricultural economy with a small modern sector and a large traditional sector. Pushed off the best land, many peasants retreated to marginal areas and continued to produce cereals and raise livestock for subsistence. Some better-off Tunisians joined the modern sector. The net results of these trends included large landholdings concentrated in fewer hands, loss of property rights for hereditary occupants, and peasant plots frequently too small and disadvantaged to sustain a family. The increasing population meant that family plots were further fragmented by inheritance. The small size of parcels made it not worthwhile to invest in modernizing existing methods of farming, fighting erosion, and so on. Reynold Dahl described the agrarian situation of dualism:

> At the time of independence in 1956, French and Italian "colon" farmers occupied 850,000 hectares of the best land in Tunisia, mostly in the North. Although this represented only one-tenth of the total cultivable land area, the European sector which accounted for one-sixteenth of the total population produced 95 per cent of the wine and 40 per cent of the cereals and accounted for one third of the total cash farm income. So the Tunisian agricul-

Table 4. Dual Agricultural Economy at Independence

Family background and number	hect. of land	Avg. farm size	Role in Economy
European: 4000 families	800,000	200 ha	Modern Sector
Tunisian: 5000 families	350,000	70 ha	Modern Sector
Tunisian: 450,000 families	3,150,000	7 ha	Traditional

Source: Dahl 1971, 32–33.

tural economy possessed the characteristics of a dual economy with a small modern sector and a large traditional sector.

The modern sector consisted of 4,000 European families owning and operating farms of an average size of 200 hectares, and about 5,000 Tunisian families owning farms averaging 70 hectares each. The great bulk of the rural population, however, was in the traditional sector which comprised 450,000 families owning an average of 7 hectares each. (Dahl 1971, 32–33)

The dual economy was particularly characteristic of the region focused on in this study. In 1956 an area of 33,426 hectares of land in the lower Medjerda Valley was surveyed. More than 23,000 hectares were taken up by large-scale farming establishments, and 7,773 hectares were owned by 284 medium-sized farms, some belonging to Tunisians and some to foreign colonialists. The small plots, owned by individual Tunisians, averaged three hectares. Data are shown in table 5.

Bardin (1965, 36) estimated that, in northern Tunisia, a minimum of eight hectares of land were needed to support a peasant family of four or five.

Increasing Peasant Impoverishment in Spite of Better Techniques, Higher Overall Production, and Increasing Marketization

The increase in aggregate production indicates that agricultural life in Tunisia benefited from the Protectorate. When France occupied Tunisia in 1881 only 600,000 hectares were under cultivation, of which 530,000 were devoted to cereals. By 1938, the area under cultivation for cereal alone was 1,300,000 hectares. The area occupied by olive trees increased from 30,000 to 550,000 hectares. Vineyards, formerly nearly nonexistent, occupied 40,000 hectares in the period just before World War II (Ziadeh 1969, 40).

Investment in underutilized land increased as French law began "rationalizing" land use by freeing some areas from archaic forms of land tenure, such

Table 5. Small Plots in the Lower Medjerda Valley

433 plots of 0-2 ha	total area 447 ha	average 1 ha
252 plots of 2-5 ha	total area 960 ha	average 3.8 ha
144 plots of 5-10 ha	total area 1093 ha	average 7.6 ha
Total: 829	plots 2500 ha	

Source: Van Dooren 1968, 70.

as habous. The French and other Europeans were partly responsible for improving work methods, increasing mechanization, introducing better seed varieties and new crops such as wine grapes, reviving the planting of fruit trees, and improving the care of livestock. A small number of Tunisians used new techniques on large-scale farms. In sum, parts of Tunisia gained modern techniques and increased their production during the Protectorate. The growing Mediterranean market, especially trade with France, also improved incentives for those able to produce crops for market, and made some of the best-placed farmers wealthy. This included a portion of the five thousand Tunisian families operating in the modern sector.

Total production of a variety of crops at the end of the Protectorate, shown in table 6 for 1955–56, indicates the dramatic gain in cereal production: 6,407,000 quintals in the year prior to independence, as compared with the figure cited above of 2,000,000 quintals in the 1880s. The modern sector was largely responsible for the general gains in cereals and other products.

The dramatic increases in agricultural production during the Protectorate were matched by the dramatic decline in standards of living for the peasantry. The alarming situation was noted by many, both in the 1940s and 1950s and more recently. Historical studies indicate that the level of rural unemployment steadily increased during the twentieth century as the rate of population growth increased, mechanization became more widespread, and foreign farmers controlled more land (Poncet 1962, 54; Cuisenier 1961). Several sources say that unemployment reached 25 percent in the 1950s (Simmons 1970, 77–78; Montmartin and Bernis 1955, 395–436). Paul Sebag (1951, 162), after attempting to amass all of the available figures, concluded that the annual average revenue of a peasant family in 1948 was twenty to twenty-five francs. As noted earlier, the consumption value available on average to the Tunisian peasantry in 1948 was one-third of that available in the 1880s (Poncet 1962, 135).

A study undertaken in 1937–38 to determine peasant nutrition in Tunisia concluded that malnutrition was widespread: 18 percent of peasants had an

Table 6. Global Production at the End of the Protectorate, 1955–56

Product	Production in quintals
Total Cereals	6,407,000
Hard Wheat	3,320,000
Soft Wheat	1,452,000
Barley	1,560,000
Maize	18,000
Oats	57,000

Product	Production in quintals
Industrial Crops	252,000
Tobacco	11,000
Cork	54,000
Olive Oil	220,000
Citrus Fruits	660,000
Dates	380,000
Wine Grapes	1,690,000
Dessert Grapes	200,000
Vegetables	2,350,000

Source: Gil 1972.

"abundant" caloric intake of 3000 calories or more per day; 15 percent had a "sufficient" intake of 2400 to 3000 calories; 11 percent were in the danger zone of 2000 to 2400 calories; 15 percent were undernourished, consuming between 1500 and 2000 calories; 22 percent were seriously undernourished, consuming 1000 to 1500 calories; and 17 percent were nearly starving, consuming less than 1000 calories per day (Sebag 1951, 163).

The general poverty of the great mass of the peasantry during the Protectorate was also evident in deteriorating housing conditions: mud huts, with roofs of branches and straw, increased while the number of brick houses declined (Sebag 1951, 163). Bidonvilles in cities, filled with recent arrivals from the countryside, multiplied and grew. These shantytowns, with their houses often made of tin or of mud and thatch, were especially evident around Tunis. Employment in industry and other sectors of the urban economy largely did not exist for their inhabitants (Dardel and Slaheddine 1955).

Dardel and Slaheddine studied the origin of the inhabitants of the bidonvilles. They were often cultivators who could no longer survive as farmers following the opening of the market; their harvests were too small to compete with modern farms. Also, fragmentation of plots made parcels unviable.

These peasants were chased from the land by forces in a modernizing agrarian economy, including mechanization and the need to lease land that they could not cultivate competitively. Soon enough this land was lost altogether:

> [These are] cultivators from Béja, Souk-el-Arba, the Medjerda Valley who were put in the position of being unable to cultivate their land either by an opening of the market, in which they could not compete due to weak harvests, or fragmentation of their parcels. . . . The biography is classic, of a small cultivator from around Béja, returning from the army, rents his land, rents himself on this land, and as soon as modernization of the enterprise is made possible by the arrival of agricultural machines, finds himself unemployed. (Dardel and Slaheddine 1955, 452–53)

Many concerned observers pointed to mechanization, especially tractors on cereal lands, as a major reason that the land could no longer provide a living for such a high proportion of the peasantry, at a time when other means of survival did not exist for most. The primary trade union in Tunisia, the UGTT, passed a resolution in 1956 requiring that mechanization on colon farms be reduced (Simmons 1970, 7).

The vast increase in production during the Protectorate clearly indicates that some people were getting wealthier, not poorer. Europeans, especially the French, reaped the main part of these benefits. Land policies during colonization served to allow colons to take control of the best agricultural land at prices scarcely more than one percent of market prices in France. Government credit and trade agreements with the home country helped create modern farms with marketable products.

Feudal elements of the beylical regime and "owners" of iqta^c concessions and habous domains also became richer during the Protectorate. Some members of this aristocracy sold their property rights to the French, or ceded habous property in enzel arrangements. Others continued to lease the land or have it cultivated in sharecropping arrangements. Gradually, however, members of this social group began to copy the colons and cultivate the soil directly, introducing modern agricultural techniques and employing salaried labor. Rural notables were better able than the peasant masses to modernize the land on which they shared property rights, obtain the credit, agricultural machines, and farming methods necessary to increase production of a variety of crops, and thrive in a growing market economy. High unemployment ensured low salaries and helped to make fortunes. The five thousand modern Tunisian farms on 350,000 hectares of prime agricultural land in 1956 attest to the development of a Tunisian agrarian bourgeoisie. Hereditary occupants of this land and of the 800,000 hectares of colonial farms lost the "right" to make a living on this soil.

The small peasantry, with insecure access to small parcels, frequently became landless and unemployed. Others made just enough to survive on family labor and represented part of the majority of the rural population, the 450,000 families with an average of seven hectares of land that they farmed with traditional methods, rarely producing the high yields or products necessary to participate in the market economy. The lack of irrigation for their properties meant that they remained at the mercy of the weather.

On the other side of the ledger, modern farms provided salaried labor. There is no reason to think that this was not a better deal for some rural dwellers, especially for the sharecroppers who obtained full-time employment and a salary. The striking counterpoint to this is that with one in four unemployed, many peasants must have lost property rights and also been unable to find employment. A modern cereal farm of 150 hectares provided permanent employment for only two or three workers and seasonal work for five or six (Marthelot 1955, 481–501). In general, seasonal salaried labor was much more common than year-round work. Some cultivators worked as seasonal laborers to supplement their income from their microparcels.

Salaried labor became a part but not the main feature of agrarian life. Family labor on family farms in the traditional sector continued to be important for peasants even as cash crops for export and technical changes in agricultural production developed around them. Salaries were low and jobs few enough that workers probably attempted to hold on to family parcels while obtaining work elsewhere whenever they were able. The rural exodus to nowhere places like the bidonvilles, challenges to peasant property, and high unemployment, as well as a decreasing ability to obtain sufficient calories, provided compelling incentives to struggle to maintain peasant institutions of kinship solidarity and mutual aid.

Income distribution (shown in table 7) supports the assertion of widespread poverty prior to the serious development efforts after independence. Village studies done in the 1960s confirm that a family income of $5 per month was not unusual (Zghal 1967a). The concentration of wealth at the extremes of the scale indicates the gulf between rich and poor.

The degree of land concentration that developed during the Protectorate further illustrates the gap between rich and poor. According to Habib Attia, in 1962 approximately 50 percent of the total agricultural population in Tunisia exploited only 7.8 percent of the land. The mechanized modern sector, which

Table 7. Income Distribution, 1961 (in U.S. Dollars)

	Number of Persons		% of Total Population		
Annual Income	Rural	Urban	Rural	Urban	Total
0–$50	1,166,000	349,000	28	9%	37%
51–75	605,000	222,000	15	5%	20%
76–100	305,000	93,000	7	2%	9%
101–125	176,000	117,000	4	3%	7%
126–150	101,000	118,000	2	3%	5%
151–175	69,000	55,000	2	1%	3%
176–200	41,000	73,000	1	2%	3%
201–225	27,000	46,000	1	1%	2%
Over 226	110,000	457,000	3	11%	14%

Source: Simmons 1970, 8

evolved largely to produce for the lucrative French market, received virtually no competition from the traditional Tunisian sector, which produced for
subsistence. Most of the cultivators of the modern sector were located in the
Northern Tell region. In this area 15 percent of the population, both European
and Tunisian, controlled 68 percent of the total land (Roberts 1976) (table 8).

The efforts of a peasantry attempting to battle the forces of land concentration are revealed in a letter sent in 1951 by the hereditary occupants of a
henchir in Tebourba to the prime minister, asserting ownership rights to the
land:

> We the undersigned, Fradj Ben Hassan Trabelesi, Tunisian, age 41, married and
> father of six children, farmer of a henchir in the sheikhat [mashyakha] of
> Tebourba; Ahmed Ben Hassan Trabelesi, Tunisian, age 45, married with eight
> children, farmer at the same place; Salah Chaouch Trabelesi, Tunisian, age
> 35, married, father of two children, with his widowed mother in his charge,
> farmer at the same place; Boubaker Ben Amara El Ayari, Tunisian, age 35, mar-
> ried, father of three children, farmer at the same place; Mansour Ben Trabelesi,
> age 46, married, father of six, farmer at the same place; Mohamed Ben Ali
> Trabelesi, Tunisian, age 35, married, father of two children and charged with
> the care of a widowed mother and three orphaned brothers, farmer at the same
> place; Mohamed Ben Salah el Ferchichi, Tunisian, age 60, father of three chil-
> dren, farmer at the same place; Bou Laarasse Ben Salah El Ferchichi, Tunisian,
> age 41, married, father of four children, farmer at the same place; Mohamed
> Ben Boubaker El Ayari, Tunisian, age 45, married, father of three children, of
> which two are married with children and live with me, farmer at the same
> place; Slimane ben Makhlouf El Gharbi, Tunisian, age 70, married, father of

Table 8. Land Distribution, 1962

Farm Size	Percent of Cultivators	Percent of Surface
under 10 hectares	63.2%	16.3%
10–50 hectares	32.6%	43.7%
over 50 hectares	4.2%	40.0%
Total	100.0%	100.0%

Source: Attia 1966, 36.

three children, farmer at the same place; Mohamed Salah Ben Boujemaa El Ayari, Tunisian, married, father of six children, farmer at the same place; Mohamed Ben Amara El Hammami, Tunisian, age 50, married, father of six children, farmer at the same place; Belgacem Ben Mohamed Darmoule, Tunisian, age 30, widowed and charged with the care of a widowed mother and three orphaned brothers; Mohamed Ben Brik Riaha, Tunisian, age 45, married, father of six children, farmer at the same place. As farmer occupants, passing the land down from father to son, we have cleared this land and fertilized the soil, giving it value; we have even planted olive groves that are actually productive and on which we pay taxes. The Department of Administration of Public Domains has made us pay rent, with which we are up to date, except for the last two years when we have been unable to find the person to whom we should pay. We have learned that the Administration of Public Domains plans to prevent us from cultivating this land and uproot us from the soil, and throw us into the countryside, men, women, the elderly, and children. (letter in the National Archives of Tunisia, 1951)

Individuals at the end of the Protectorate were restrained from breaking away from a moral economy by blood relationships, customs, increasing impoverishment, and lack of opportunities in the modern sector. Tribal links were weakened during the development of modern private property and a central administration better able to act on its needs in all areas of the country. However, the use of "sheikhat," a tribal division, to designate an administrative area in this letter indicates the continued importance of these geographical entities, kinship, and traditional leaders such as shuykh at the dawn of independence.

Deterioration and Revival of a Moral Economy

Obviously, the penetration of markets, French colonial rule, and the independent Tunisian state have had a tremendous impact on the traditional forms of social organization described above. More and more people are trying to maximize their individual profits, and the moral economies found in different communities have deteriorated. Still, the networks of support, exchange, and interaction among groups connected by blood, community, religion, and other affinities have partially survived the onslaught of colonialism and post-independence rural politics, especially in the lower social strata.

Also, during the initial cooperative period of the 1960s a combination of state efforts and strategies of the small peasantry combined to maintain many aspects of traditional social organization. At the time, the remnants of tribal structure survived in most of Tunisia. The names of tribes, sections of tribes, and sections of these sections affected social structure. The values of the segmentary system remained. One study claimed that 30 to 50 percent of the marriages in the Tunisian countryside were between first cousins, an obvious signal of kinship solidarity (Zghal 1967a, 100). Living in the margins of the modern economy, most Tunisian peasants relied heavily on patron-client relations in agricultural production and rural community life. Since the time of the work camps, they had been growing more likely to wait for things out of their control: for rain in unirrigated areas and aid from the state. The cooperatives could be adapted to all of these patterns.

According to Abdelkader Zghal (1967b, 103), the first contact that administrators had with future cooperative participants was made according to the norms of traditional authority. It was the shaykh, traditional authority, that convoked peasants to aid topographers in delimiting the borders of the cooperatives. At the first stage, no one explained the reason for the operations; the shaykh merely called them a "government project."

The cooperative system began to function according to the norms of the traditional system. In all of the northern cooperatives, it was the shuykh who suggested the first lists of ordinary cooperative workers and higher-ranking participants. They would generally compose two lists of candidates for specialized positions: one based on technical skills, and one based on the most important families in the region, especially their own (Zghal 1967b, 104). This continuation of social rank belied the role of cooperatives as agents of change.

Other compromises by cooperative administrators indicate that the project's hoped-for social changes would lose out to tradition. Many of the new houses built on cooperatives were distributed according to ethnic grouping, not alphabetical order. This helped to maintain the solidarity of kinship groupings. In addition the farm animals, so important as security, were housed and fed on the cooperatives and allowed to spend the nights next to the cooperative participants' homes.

Mira Zussman offered a very interesting detailed example of how cooperative participants in Tebourba could impose peasant traditions on the operation
of a state farm:

> The combined households of the brothers grew until over fifty members of
> the douar, or hamlet, lived at the heart of the agro-combinat. They maintained
> their own farm animals . . . and a flock that ranged between thirty and fifty
> sheep. Four of the brothers rented a private parcel which belonged to the
> Hadj's farm next door. The rental was fi-shshtar; i.e., divided in two. The
> owner supplied the land, seed, fertilizer, equipment, and transportation—
> the brothers supplied the labor. At harvest time, the Hadj and the brothers split
> the profits equally. In this manner, they were able to maintain both an indi-
> vidual and collective income. Cooperation within the family extended beyond
> farming and the tending of sheep. The wives characteristically worked to-
> gether and with the children's participation; they were engaged in sewing,
> baking khubz tabouna (traditional bread cooked in a mud oven), and rolling
> the year's supply of couscous, as well as in working in the Hadj's fields. One
> of the wives was a fine potter who provided each household and other neigh-
> bors with earthenware casseroles, incense burners, and kanouns.
>
> The brothers superimposed their kin-based economy on the formal struc-
> ture of the agro-combinat as if the latter did not exist. Si Hamadi summed up
> the difference between family collective and state farms or cooperatives con-
> cisely. "Brothers work well together, strangers do not." Family cooperation en-
> tailed trust, state farms did not. (Zussman 1992, 136)

In sum, social organization on cooperatives reflected compromises between
cooperative ideals and peasant traditions; but the traditions, overall, seemed to
carry the day in many localities. It makes little sense to reduce rural social organization in Tunisia in the 1960s to individual maximizing strategies. Village
studies confirm this. They also reveal that various factors, such as the history of
particular regions, market forces, and the state, can all have an impact on social
structure (Boukra 1976; Huxley 1990; Duvignaud 1970; Zahra 1982; Simmons
1974; Hopkins 1983; Zghal 1967a). The Sahel coastal region had a history of private family property, village life, and entrepreneurship. Large-scale confiscation of land by the French and cooperativization was most vigorously fought
there, and village studies of the region indicate that rational actor theory, with
its emphasis on the individual, was more applicable there than elsewhere.

Where cooperatives held sway in Tunisia, their privatization bridged old and
new land tenure issues. Before the Protectorate, rights over these lands were
contested by various elites and peasant cultivating communities. The French
confiscated this fertile soil during colonization. The state took over from the

Table 9. Cooperatives Leased in Tebourba since 1991

Leased Cooperatives	Hectares
SMVDA Bourg Toumi	800
Tongor	265
El Bouruka	588
S Verged	670
El Amra	120
B.T. El Batan	15
CPPS Mehrine	55
S. Khangot	448
S. Plaine D'Or	478
Sodac Chougi	601

Remaining Cooperatives	Hectares
U.C.P. Dekhlia	1480
U.C.P. Lansarine	1100
U.C.P. Mallaha	1400
Total Hectares:	8020

Source: unpublished table, Tebourba Office Of Agricultural Extension, 1994.

French at independence, while the descendants of the rural notables and squatters with ancestral links to the land waited for state land policy to determine the final winners of this multigenerational struggle over property rights.

Market reforms in the north (the privatization of cooperatives among them) and intensive state involvement in transforming the communities of this area raise the question of how rural social organization adapts itself to state-led economic liberalization in a region where cultural traditionalism has demonstrated persistence. The full case study of Tebourba in the next chapter will reveal how, in order to head off equity concerns, state agents have promoted the reactivation of traditional clientelism and the Islamic welfare mechanisms described in this chapter. The small peasantry have withdrawn from formal politics and become more enmeshed in patron-client ties. Still, there remains perceptible volatility beneath the emerging social arrangements. Evidence suggests that subordinate groups are not always in the thrall of the neo-traditional social order, even as the narrowing of employment opportunities and access to land join with elite strategies to channel their economic and political behavior along traditional lines.

The inequities of market reforms in Tebourba have been stark and indisputable. Table 9 lists the cooperatives privatized since 1991. All contracts went to large farmers, many with ancestral ties to the old beylical regime. The three remaining cooperatives are being considered for privatization.

❖ 4 ❖

NEO-TRADITIONALISM IN TEBOURBA

FIRST SETTLED BY farmers from Andalusia, Tebourba has been home to a community for over five hundred years. Rolling hills full of olive trees line one side of the town. The flat plains are covered with wheat fields, fruit trees, and vegetable gardens. Farming is done next to houses in town and in surrounding areas. The Medjerda River, whose source is located in Algeria, provides irrigation.

An understanding of local politics in Tebourba can begin with a description of my visit to the délégué. His office is located in a white cinderblock compound on the outskirts of the old *medina*, or city. An elderly man in traditional dress greeted me and offered me a chair and tea for the long wait involved in any effort to meet with the town's understandably busy highest-ranking official. A handmade poster on the wall indicated the approaching deadline for presenting titles to land on the outskirts of cooperatives scheduled to be turned over to private management. While waiting, I was moved from room to room down a hallway where low-ranking bureaucrats inquired about the reason for my visit and greeted friends and acquaintances.

During almost all working hours this is a bustling place. Farmers from outside the town center come in to voice grievances about the widespread lack of land titles, which hinders efforts to obtain credit, or with simpler concerns, like obtaining a birth certificate. In a general way, this has become a place to make demands of the patron state. Though most people claim that they have gotten very little from the state, nearly all can cite occasions when they have gone directly to the délégué to request such things as financial help for a sick relative or that their status as a cooperative worker be passed down to their offspring. It is well known that a much higher percentage of requests are granted at election time.

Eventually I was summoned to the délégué's office. It is enormous and slightly regal in furnishing, with the délégué's large red felt chair as the centerpiece. The délégué informed me right away that everything in this town is his business and province. We discussed community solidarity and the délégué's awareness of minor and major events in town. During two of my three visits, he pointedly placed a call to the governor. The gesture emphasized the concentric circles of state power. Poor informants have recounted stories of being treated with contempt for daring to ask for a favor, and also tales of empathy, involving for instance the rapid delivery of an expensive medicine. At least once a week, the délégué's office is used for meetings with Tebourba's ⁽umad.

A community with Tebourba's longevity develops an identity that can be discovered by examining the expectations that community members have of one another. In contemporary times community norms still provide a set of expectations. The rules of behavior in Tebourba are sometimes ignored, but are followed widely enough to reveal themselves to the outside observer. First, in desperate times one can turn to extended family members for help to survive. Second, the wealthy provide a range of goods and services to the poor: employment, gifts of grain and other agricultural products during the harvest and during the Islamic festivals of Ramadan, al⁽Eid al-Kabir and al⁽Eid as-Saghir; the use of their land for grazing; and, in the cases of loyal clients, loans and intermediation in economic and bureaucratic transactions. The poorest of the poor are to receive alms and the zakat from the wealthy and the middle class. Third, the poor provide the wealthy with labor services at low cost, and grant prestige and high social standing to those who follow the second rule. Last, people keep a mental account of favors granted, whether large or small, and reciprocate when possible. Related to this, community members are expected to continuously build up their connections and relations with people both within and outside the community.

The actions of state officials in Tebourba fit into these traditional patterns of behavior. State patronage serves as another means for the poor to solicit resources in exchange for their support of more powerful people. The Islamic welfare mechanisms would have been much less effective by now, due to the free-rider problem associated with public goods, if party officials did not pressure the wealthy to keep contributing to these mechanisms of redistribution and legitimation of wealth.

The traditional community norms described above evolved largely in a pre-market era when many peasants produced mainly for subsistence. The lack of mechanization in farming made the labor services of the poor more crucial then they are today. In addition, over the years migration from other areas has made the population of Tebourba more heterogenous. In spite of these social changes, residents of the community, both new and old, maintain a social identity based largely on adherence to traditional institutions.

Tebourbans identify themselves as a community. They have a conscious model of community, which they express linguistically in the word "Tebourbi." In Arabic the addition of the *nisba*—a suffixed *i*—creates another word describing the possessor of certain qualities or a member of a group. Local jokes hold that immigrants to Tebourba will refer to themselves as Tebourbi seconds after their arrival in order to take advantage of the mechanisms of redistribution of wealth. The "real" Tebourbi of Andalusian descent may resemble each other more, they may intermarry more often; but newcomers can share in the community's common beliefs, values, customs, and behavior.

To describe Tebourba as a community does not imply isolation. Tebourbi are part of a Tunisian social, economic, and political order. To be Tebourbi is to participate in local allocations of wealth, power, and social standing, but community membership does not prevent people from also participating in the larger arena. Individuals pursue their interests wherever they lead. Some people migrate to Tunis or elsewhere and maintain ties of interdependence with relatives in Tebourba. The town's proximity to Tunis even permits commuting to jobs in the capital. Thus the social structure of Tebourba is more fluid than the concept of community suggests. Still, residents of the territorial entity of Tebourba usually participate in elaborate forms of social exchange and rituals of redistribution within the community.

There is an Islamic quality to life in Tebourba, which finds expression particularly in the purification of wealth through almsgiving during Islamic festivals. The tenacity of Islamic welfare mechanisms even during the creation of a market economy is partly due to the religious nature of these traditional social forms. They are maintained through the regular observance of religious practices, the socialization of children in families, and in this case the efforts of local political officials.

A community study cannot avoid the issue of conflicts among socioeconomic classes. Many analysts, myself included, have described rural communities in North Africa as tied together by networks of relationships and elaborate forms of social exchange. Patron-client ties, kinship relations, community traditions, Islamic social norms, and other factors supposedly link members of different socioeconomic groups together in a way that lessens the possibility of the development of economic classes pitted against one another in a combat over material resources.

Still, it is clear that if we define class without reference to class consciousness and conflict, then we can view Tebourba in class terms. Doing so draws attention to inequality in the distribution of wealth, prestige, and power. For the most part, there are indigenous terms for this hierarchy. At the bottom are the poorest community members, who if left to their own devices might not survive. They are called "the below zeros" or "the squeezed." Agricultural workers without secure employment drift in and out of this category. Thus, in a community where agricultural work is usually seasonal, the below zeros constitute the majority. The middle peasants, with secure access to enough land to provide for a family that supplies the farm's labor force, are commonly referred to as "men who stand on their own two feet." To obtain a family farm is to become a man (*rajil*). People who have enough resources to hire others or rent large amounts of land are called simply the well-off. From here on, I will use the terms "below zeros," "middle peasants," and "well-off" to name the basic strata of the rural community.

As the administrative capital of this agricultural region, Tebourba is a growing town with jobs in administration, commerce, construction, and education, among other fields. Still, farming is the dominant activity, and the one that we will primarily deal with here. The well-off may own hundreds of hectares of land or use the most modern techniques on holdings of as little as twenty to thirty hectares, and their profits may exceed a hundred thousand dollars a year.[1] Members of this group have the closest social relations with government officials. Some of this group invest in activities outside of farming, but they usually hire others to manage these operations.

The below zeros are basically agricultural laborers who have a lot of difficulty obtaining secure, year-around employment. As a survival strategy, they diversify their productive activities by engaging in petty commerce and construction. Frequently they migrate to urban areas, where they may or may not find gainful employment. Their numbers may include owners of microparcels who produce wheat for subsistence and may own a few olive trees and farm animals. Obtaining the yearly food supply, the ʿawula, is of paramount importance for this group. Traditional institutions of mutual aid and redistribution are an important part of this effort.

State Agents and the Moral Economy

During economic reform, local political elites try to create more legitimacy for state policy by reinforcing the channels of a moral economy based on an

---

1. This information comes from personal interviews. Interviewees were more likely to underestimate than overestimate their income.

Islamic hierarchy for allocating resources. The ʿumad themselves described to
me the party's efforts to maintain community welfare mechanisms by coordi-
nating with wealthy landowners. This ʿumda (quoted in chapter 1) was a former member of the National Guard:

> The poor are reluctant to ask for aid. The ʿumda meets with party members
> who try to figure out who needs help and what to present. Several sector
> heads will meet with their ʿumda and during alʿEid al-Kabir, alʿEid as-Saghir,
> Ramadan, and other holidays they distribute the aid. We get the assistance
> from the wealthy, who are friends of the party. Some of the rich give directly to
> the poor. On religious holidays some people will give around thirteen dinars to
> a poor family, or a sack of wheat. Since I've been here we've had good commu-
> nity solidarity. There was some trouble a year or so ago and they talked about
> building a National Guard office across the street. However, after I worked to-
> gether with the rich to help out the poor, things quieted down. Just this year
> there were eighty gift packages given out during Ramadan in my sector.

Another ʿumda:

> During the harvest there is a lot of solidarity between the rich and poor. Dur-
> ing Ramadan money is given out, or oil, sugar, and wheat. Clothes and meat
> are given on holidays. During alʿEid al-Kabir lambs and goats are given to the
> poor. Party members go around to the rich and we see that sometimes a rich
> person will give a whole animal to a poor family. Many of them give the ani-
> mals to me to give to the poor. Some give up to four sheep. Hajj Elloumi built
> an entire mosque. Three other large farmers bought a mosque. We have people
> who give land for a hospital.

A third ʿumda:

> There are strong connections in this sector. The rich think of the poor auto-
> matically. When times are hard, the state will meet with the wealthy and get
> assistance to distribute to the poor. During the first ten days of Ramadan and
> the last ten days the rich give to the poor. During alʿEid al-Kabir lambs are
> given, as well as something during the small festival at the end of Ramadan.
> We get a lot of help for the poor. Party leaders have an account where people
> can give the zakat. Many people give one-tenth, which we distribute to the
> poor. Ibn Toumi left an inheritance from his olive oil enterprise for the poor.
> We gave twenty-five portions of five liters each to the poor.

In addition to providing direct aid to the poor, some ʿumad hope that the
privatization of cooperatives will reinvigorate the now-diffuse patron-client
ties that were part of an earlier moral economy:

The state failed with cooperatives because they organized laborers and managers poorly. The cooperatives are impersonal; they cannot help the poor in urgent situations like death in the family. The Hajj can help the people who work for him because he has a personal relationship. His workers are happier than when they worked on cooperatives. He helps them get their ʿawula [yearly provisions gathered around harvest time. This is especially important for the many agricultural workers who do not work year-round. The ʿawula usually consists of flour, oil, sugar, harissa, and spices]. At harvest time, the Hajj sells wheat to his workers at wholesale prices. In addition, he always gives the zakat.

The Hajj doesn't have technical training, but he is a specialist at growing wheat. Even without irrigation, his wheat does well. At a glance, he can pick out the best-quality seeds that people with degrees miss. His wheat is used as a model all over the country. That's why he was given the cooperative lands of wheat fields. The Hajj's two sons run the place alone; they do the work of twenty administrators.

Local party officials have long involved themselves in traditional and non-traditional community allocation patterns. This is not a new phenomenon. As Eric Wolf points out, "The sharing of resources within communal organizations and reliance on ties with powerful patrons were recurrent ways in which peasants strove to reduce risks and to improve their stability, and both were condoned and frequently supported by the state" (Wolf 1969, 279).

The Poor: The Below Zeros, the Squeezed

> Oh arm that digs wells from rocks
> Oh arm that moves trees and earth
> Oh arm that's busy at work for what gain of the harvest
> All my years decrease as they fill with work
> All my life since I was small
> Always selling myself, we wait for things to get better
> My grandfather, my uncle, my father died and left only pictures
> They destroyed mountains and left, leaving me only palm carpets
> —Song of Tebourba agricultural workers

The "below zeros" or the "squeezed" can be found in their mud huts surrounded by a fence of olive trees that sit beside more permanent dwellings, or in the cinderblock sprawl that sits alongside the thousand-hectare holdings of one of the community's wealthiest residents. Those with small parcels or temporary agricultural work—jobs can last as little as two weeks—may be found in the fields. Their comments reveal that they are not often utility maximizers, but are, rather, embedded in patterns of producing and distributing resources that reflect extended family solidarity, community-wide elaborate social relations, and dependence on bureaucratic and Islamic welfare mechanisms.

However, even as their behavior indicates that many are following moral economy channels revived by political elites, the hegemony of this elite social vision may be shaky.[2] My interviews indicate that the small peasantry seem to be following viable political and economic strategies while harboring a great deal of anger at new economic arrangements. These emerging social arrangements increasingly privilege rural notables while designating many of the peasants as welfare recipients in an explicitly Islamic hierarchy. On the other hand, the Islamic nature of the social order makes it sensible for both poor Muslims in crisis and wealthier Muslims seeking to legitimize their increasing riches to revitalize traditional institutions.

The poor population in Tebourba is numerous. Poverty can be measured by calculating the cost of food and other basic consumables (the poverty line) and comparing it to actual expenditure. Using household consumption surveys, Tunisia's National Institute of Statistics (INS) has set the poverty line at 185 Tunisian dinars per year in rural areas (as this book went to press, one dinar was worth about US$0.73). I define the rural poor in a more general way by using the same definition that I have used for the small peasantry: those with insecure access to land and employment who have trouble obtaining the resources to keep themselves and their families "above zero." This definition calls attention to a threshold of resources that many people struggle to get that may or may not be included in official government numbers for the poor. For example, I include the new poor of released cooperative workers and seasonal laborers, who may or may not be able to obtain employment from season to season.

Some of these people have migrated to the region recently, from the more impoverished and drought-plagued south. Other families have been residents for generations. Overwhelmingly, it is a population of agricultural laborers, who at best find employment for six months of the year. Often, every able body, mother, father, and children, attempts to work in the fields in order to make ends meet. A lucky few may find work in light construction or in the capital, Tunis, which is thirty miles away.

For this income group especially, the privatization of cooperatives constitutes a crisis. Work in cooperatives meant year-round employment, with health

---

2. Building on Gramsci's notion of hegemony, James Scott (1985) discusses the "weapons of the weak," with which they can protest new, disadvantageous social arrangements.

and retirement benefits. Sometimes homes were built on the cooperatives, and livestock could graze on their land. When the cooperatives were turned over to private control, these privileges had to be renegotiated. In private hands, the cooperative farmland became more capital-intensive, and many workers were released with few other ways to earn an income. Frequently, they turned to relatives, friends, patrons, and traditional institutions to survive. Even people who were not cooperative workers have been hard hit by the reforms. Cooperative workers contributed resources to many others, bolstering their stability, and the fired workers have heightened the competition for increasingly scarce agricultural work.

One laborer, Nur Eddine, earns sixty dinars a month cultivating five hectares of land for an absentee landlord. At thirty-three years of age, he has four small children and is the sole supporter of his elderly parents. His only brother is unemployed and Nur Eddine helps his family out when he can. Other people in the community viewed him as a very capable farmer. Nur Eddine strongly conveyed his desire for his own piece of property, and how unfair he considered part-time labor:

> How could they give all that [former cooperative] land to those people? If I had one hectare, I could produce more than five or six hectares' worth. I work summer and fall only. How can I live on six months of work? For example, I may work one week or two weeks with a cow owner until he sells the milk, and then I have to hit the road. He has twenty thousand dinars and I have ten dinars. I have a brain like you and him. Why is it that workers always stay workers? I can't help my children improve. If you work for someone you have to pay for clothes and food, but when the work runs out, what then? My parents live with me and sometimes I just can't make it.

> My boss may have thirty thousand dinars and when I ask for a loan I may get twenty dinars. Why should someone live below zero while others drive expensive cars? He uses you. He doesn't pay you on time. The owner's wealth, even his cars came from us. I have a brain and blood and I work, but I can't even buy boots for the winter's rain. My brother has a diploma but he can't get a job. We don't know the right people for those kinds of jobs. All those years of going to school were wasted. He tried for a job but the son of a neighbor got it, and he didn't have a diploma. You have to have the right connections. It's the same with farming work. There is so much competition that people only hire people that they know or that their good workers tell them about.

Ibrahim, whom I quote next, is a farmer and a second-generation resident of Tebourba; his family came from Sidi Bou Zid in the south. His father rented five hectares of land from the same man for most of his working life. Now fifty-two, Ibrahim has only been able to hold on to two hectares. His life is a constant search for the funds to rent more land and pay for irrigation, but he is continually priced out of the market. Four grown children live and work with Ibrahim. With their families, they share one budget. They grow olives and vegetables, which they sell in Tebourba and occasionally in Tunis.

When possible, Ibrahim's two sons work as laborers for four dinars a day. Thirteen people live in the house with him, and he saw little chance that his married children would move out in the near future. The day of the interview we sat under an olive tree near the three sheep that made up his herd. Ibrahim kept eyeing the field next door. The widow who lived there left several hectares uncultivated, but refused to rent to him. Even as he said this, he kept repeating that he couldn't afford it anyway. In a matter of a few years the rent of his two hectares has risen from 150 to 500 dinars a year. Making this point, he went on in a bit of a tirade:

> You know that the rich farmers only pay twenty-five dinars a hectare for the cooperatives. They might as well give it away. They give old men contracts for fifty years. How can Hicham, who is in his sixties, farm when he's 110 years old? It's impossible to rent if you're poor. It's not like it was with Nouria [who was prime minister in the 1970s]; you need connections now to get anything from the administration. Even for water, if you know someone in one administration you have to get them to talk to the people in the other administration. The rich are starting to keep everything for themselves. The farmers' union is for the rich, so I never ask them for anything. Still, we don't make enough to live on anymore.
>
> You may get aid from the rich, but they do it to manipulate you. They don't want you to work for another boss who may pay you more. We get some aid from the rich whom we know, so we don't have to beg others for work. Whatever they give is to help with their social image, so we are helping them as well. The state seems to be helping them the most. Privatization is bad for small farmers and the poor because we aren't getting anything. There are a lot more unemployed people and some people are leaving Tebourba completely. They can't make it here.

In tight financial times Ibrahim uses a strategy of extended family solidarity to produce and distribute resources. He is cynical about aid from the rich, but appears to accept it with the understanding that it is an exchange: aid for social standing. The changes in the market during economic reform appear to him as a government shift toward helping the wealthy. He expressed a growing alienation from the local governmental administration and the farmers' union.

High rents and water prices make it difficult to participate independently in the market. The outright purchase of privatized cooperative land, much of which has become available, is quite impossible. Ibrahim is most disheartened by the low rents that the new private managers of state land are paying.

Samir is a fifty-three-year-old agricultural laborer. Presently he is unemployed. None of his four adult children has been able to find stable employment, though, like him, they find some seasonal work in agriculture. His family relies heavily on the zakat and religious gift-giving for their yearly food. He lives in a slum behind the wheat fields of a wealthy farmer, Hajj Elloumi. Hajj Elloumi received an eight-hundred-hectare contract under the privatization program. Like most of the poor, Samir is against cooperatives; his solution, which is echoed by many other poor farmers, is to give the land, in five-hectare plots, to the poor:

> Ben Salah destroyed the country and left. He knocked the hats off people [a gesture that is considered very rude]. Lambs and goats were sold for five dinars. He ripped out by the roots olive trees, which had been growing for years. We didn't have anything to lose; even my little dog died. [Because of the way they are discussed in the Koran, some Muslims consider dogs filthy and worthless.]

Despite his hostility to Ben Salah's socialist project (and Samir is one of the poor whom the minister probably wanted to help most), he is also extremely unhappy with the current reform program:

> Cooperatives didn't organize the land well. Private owners care more and they do better. However, why should the state hurt everybody and help only people like Hajj Elloumi? Half the families in this neighborhood have someone who was fired from the cooperative when Hajj Elloumi took over. He kept a few workers and fired the others. They didn't do anything. In order to get rid of them, he accused them of burning the land. He also accused the fired people of stealing. They are going to court for this, and it's nonsense. There are people who have a right to land but don't get it. You have to help them. That's why we call the rich stingy and whatnot. You know this without my telling you. The poor have a right to aid. God knows this.
>
> During the harvest some of them give the zakat. Even Hajj Elloumi gives that. For small farmers, it's enough to feed the family. Before, it was a lot better. The rich used to get together and help the needy: they would buy a tent, give a little piece of land, goats and sheep, and some wheat. It's finished now. They only give a little bit of flour.
>
> Times are really bad now because we haven't had any rain. We're asking God

for rain more than the rich. When it's bad for them it's worse for us. When the harvest is bad due to lack of rain, the state will reimburse them for the loss. If the rain comes or not it's the same for the rich.

The truth is that large farmers exploit laborers. They stand over you to keep you from stopping work. I work twelve hours a day for four dinars. I work from seven in the morning to seven at night. I was sick for eleven days, and even though I was sick and worked anyway, I haven't got my four dinars for the last day. There's a problem for laborers. For twenty years or more we work the land, yet we stay laborers. At times, my family is dying of hunger, and we have never been able to buy even two meters of land.

Hayat is a fourteen-year-old laborer. She, her father, and her mother work in agriculture in different places. Each of them earns about a hundred dinars a year, working when they can. There are seven children in the family and Hayat is the oldest. Her father forced her to leave school and help support the family. The family lives in a house built by the government next to a cooperative. Her father lost his place on a cooperative when it was privatized in the 1970s, but didn't have a lease to the small parcel that he had farmed before it was integrated into the cooperative. Hayat's biggest complaint was the size of her family, which makes it impossible for her parents to support them. Traditional institutions are an important part of the family's strategy to obtain resources. Still a child, although with adult responsibilities, she had little to say about new agricultural policies and the economic changes going on around her. She despaired of her parents' ability to provide for her and give her more choices in life:

> We get a lot of our ʿawula during the harvest, but not everyone who should give does. Some people don't give anything. Other people will give you two bags of wheat instead of ten. During the holidays we get some help and clothes. At the end of Ramadan, the smallest amount someone will give you is 600 millimes [one dinar = 1000 millimes]. I like the rich because I work for them. I can only do well if they are doing well. Sometimes we work less than six months of the year. What would we do without rich people?

Majoub is a sixty-year-old farmer who has worked for years on a few hectares of land owned by his in-laws. In addition to supporting his wife and children, he gives money, clothes, and vegetables to his first cousins. He emphasizes that the rich are less committed than they used to be to a moral economy:

> I used to live in Meja, but had problems and came here. My in-laws invited me to live and work with them. They gave me a small house and this piece of land. We don't have a lot but we help each other out. In the past the rich were

kind. If they knew someone did not have clothes and food, then they would go find them to help them out. At harvest time, everyone helped out. Sometimes the rich would give you a piece of land and allow you to use their tractors.

Times have changed. Morality has changed. The rich don't feel anything for the needy. They even fear the poor. They don't want the poor living near them or having land near them because they will ask for things. They don't even want the poor to raise a chicken near them because it would sneak on their land. Hajj Naouar, who lives next door, wants us all to move. His workers only work the land [and do not farm for themselves]. He said, "Don't raise your animals and let them eat my grass." Some of his workers had to sell their cows and look for other work. All he does is give the zakat. It's probably the full one-tenth, but that's it.

I can't understand why the government didn't help the poor with that land. A man and his family can live on five hectares. Small farmers wanted a little land to live on. It's mainly who you know. Connections are very important around here. Even in agriculture, you can hardly get a job without knowing somebody.

Hadi is an agricultural laborer who has found steady employment on one of the privatized cooperatives. He is among the middle peasants, but is included here because of his sympathy for the small peasantry and insistence that his job is not secure. At forty-one years of age he supports two small children. His nuclear family appears self-contained, though he is a strong believer in the righteousness of the Islamic welfare mechanisms:

> Small farmers are being run out of farming. The government doesn't want to divide the land into small parts. They are distributing it hundreds of hectares at a time, so the poor can't afford it. Wealthy people—it doesn't matter where they got their money, they can be lawyers, doctors, or whatever—will go to the ʿumda and plan on getting the land in one person's hands. Later they will divide the money with the ʿumda. I know that they aren't using technical criteria for the land, because people like me who studied agriculture can't get any.
>
> The rich will still help the poor some, even some of the people who I just told you about. At harvest and during the festivals, the Destour [he refers to the party by its pre-1987 name] and the ʿumda will give a little something. As far as the rich go, if the ancestors helped the poor, the kids will too.

Rached is a young man of twenty-eight. Agricultural work has been so unsteady for him that he is turning to construction and other possible jobs. He lives with his parents, but feels that he is a heavy burden on their resources:

Agricultural programs need to help the young with things like tractors and credit. Instead, everything goes to the rich. When they started "selling" the cooperatives, only the rich knew about it. Ben Salah tried to lessen class differences. What we need is a combination of Ben Salah and Nouria, something that is government-controlled to help the poor people from being run over by the rich. Poor people need to participate in politics. We need to run people in elections. Right now the rich run all of politics. The large farmers own the farmers' union and run all of the political activities.

We get through by depending on our family. The extended family is close even when you live far away. If you don't help your own, people will talk about you. There's a lot of social pressure. The nicer rich people will allow our animals to graze on their land, but there aren't enough of them.

Other poor people have a warmer view of the rich. Many of the people quoted below are in patronage relations with particular wealthy farmers. It is interesting that patron and client are usually rich and poor members of the same lineage group. I found Munir grazing his small herd of sheep on the land of Hajj Elloumi, one of the large landowners who had recently leased the land of a cooperative. At sixty years old Munir raised sheep, and when necessary sought out other agricultural work. As a distant cousin of Hajj Elloumi, he was reasonably assured of temporary work in times of need. He supported one grown son and his very elderly mother:

> I never have to worry about grass for my animals. Hajj Elloumi is the first person to help the poor. He has a tender heart. I haven't worked in the fields for over a year now, but I know that I can go to him when I need work. He is known around here for helping everybody. During Ramadan, he will slaughter sheep and give the meat to people from miles around. The land you asked about should have been spread around to the rich. They know how to farm, and would have helped more of the poor. The government can make them give work to people.

Qasem is another distant relative of Hajj Elloumi. His relatively comfortable life is secure as long as the bond with his patron is strong:

> The cooperatives needed to be privatized. If you own the land, you will work it better. This improves production. On the cooperatives, the olive trees were not even being pruned. The birds would eat the food. You should see the place since Hajj Elloumi took over. People say the Hajj and the other Elloumis get everything. You can see that I'm an Elloumi, yet I'm poor.

In general, remarkably few of the very poor could be described as working to maximize their private wealth by their own efforts. Social exchange is elaborate and mutual aid is common, especially within the extended family. On the other hand, when discussing general community behavior, most people will say that it is "every man for himself." There is general agreement that the wealthy could be doing more. This claim is usually made while comparing community solidarity and the generosity of rich peasants today to the situation one or more generations back. This comparison fits with the interpretation of James Scott (1985), who discusses the battle between rich and poor in the discourse of a rural community. The poor speak of the ancient generosity of the rich in order to press their current claims for justice, during a period of economic setbacks.

However, my interpretation differs from Scott's by pointing out that in this case, unlike in the green revolution in rural Malaysia, the state is shoring up the moral economy. State agents have made considerable efforts to prevent the wealthy from abandoning traditional welfare obligations. On the local level, it is the obligation of both activists in the hegemonic RCD party and officials of the Ministry of the Interior, including the délégué and the ʿumad, to maintain social control and political calm. These administrators and party activists use a variety of means to maintain a calm façade for their superiors, especially on occasions when state policy might hurt some groups. These means include redistribution of resources through Islamic welfare mechanisms, bureaucratic welfare payments (also controlled by state agents), and outright repression.

One result of the poor's comparing ideal generosity with current realities is that is difficult to tell how committed the rich actually are to the welfare of the poor. It is impossible to find precise counts over time of how many have participated in Islamic welfare mechanisms, and to what extent. I suspect that local officials' prodding of the rich to maintain traditional obligations has led to much more redistribution than otherwise would have been the case. This prodding is especially intense when the poor are making more economic and social demands, such as when they lose work on the cooperatives. One thing is certain: the current strategies of the poor in Tebourba to obtain and distribute resources diverge greatly from a rational actor model.

This is the case in spite of the fact that most cite the market model, with a man working for himself on his own land, as the ideal. In order to realize this ideal, they need opportunities, resources, and the skill to both produce for the market and negotiate with the administration; the small peasantry lack these attributes. Fumbled attempts to take this route lead them to return to better-known and more dependable strategies, such as reliance on traditional institutions, kinship ties, and powerful patrons.

The remarks of the délégué illustrate the striking degree to which the RCD affects social organization and maintains the viability of Islamic welfare mechanisms:

> We meet with the rich on a regular basis, because Tebourba is known for its solidarity. Aid is given to the poor during alᶜEid al-Kabir and alᶜEid as-Saghir. In fact there are eight occasions of gifts to the poor. We have religious and state holidays, and extra efforts are also made at the beginning of the school year. It is my job to be aware of things, to shift things around.

The Well-Off

Few of the wealthy live in the old medina, or traditional section of town. They build large homes along the newer streets. Many of them have satellite dishes to capture the latest European programs. Some of the fenced-in homes could justifiably be called mansions, looking as luxurious as homes in the wealthiest American neighborhoods. Concentration of wealth is a striking feature of Tebourba. The area is known for large landowners. During interviews I saw a room with a gold telephone and households with more than ten cars and trucks, in addition to motorbikes for most family members and important employees, and twenty-four-hour guards. Quick trips to Italy and France are common for the income group that other residents refer to in Arabic as the well-off.

Wealthy residents who missed out on contracts for cooperatives can be critical of the privatization plan, though they have not broken ranks and formed a general alliance with other income groups. They tend to view the poor in the same negative terms as the people who obtained the contracts. All appear to have open lines of communication with the délégué and the eight ᶜumad of the town. Two of the ᶜumad are wealthy landowners, and one wealthy landowner is a former ᶜumda. An eight-hundred-hectare cooperative was leased to the brother of an ᶜumda. The farmers' union, which meets infrequently, is viewed locally as the exclusive province of the wealthy. This group would meet informally in the market, and in one particular town café. Other evidence of coordination between the wealthy and local officials includes the phone calls directly to the délégué that invariably occurred during my visits.

More than anything else, members of this group are characterized by their control of resources. Their personal styles, family background, estate sizes, crops, and agricultural techniques vary, but they all control enough resources to be able to respond to the changes in agricultural incentives, prices, and the general economic environment caused by structural adjustment. Still, not all of them do so respond; some have and some have not.

Hajj Elloumi, who has figured prominently in this analysis, recently turned over the operation of his three-hundred-hectare personal holdings and eight-hundred-hectare cooperative lease to his two eldest sons. They grow fruit, vegetables, and wheat for sale in Tunis and Tebourba. The members of this family have been important landowners for generations, and even managed to increase their holdings during the colonial era. Hajj Elloumi, who is sixty-seven, inherited over one hundred hectares from his father. Once the French left, he managed to take over one of the most profitable French enterprises. Today the family lives in one of the homes built by a French farmer. The response of one of his sons to queries about government agricultural policies emphasized that they brought benefits to the country, but his claims of increasing employment are outright inaccuracies. Privatization of this cooperative meant the loss of over 50 percent of the customary labor days:

> The privatization program is designed to help the country: production is improved and it increases work for the people. Production was very low when we took over. Today we are producing at 80 percent of capacity. This means that the workers are happy. You have to remember that workers are selfish. If you're not careful, they won't work.

The two sons and their families share with the father the production and distribution of resources. They claim that they give agricultural products and other aid to first cousins and more distant relatives on a regular basis. The sons acknowledge that the family and close associates are tied together to get ahead. "You can't achieve goals alone. We are a close family. One hand claps for the other." Several people described Hajj Elloumi's custom of slaughtering dozens of sheep during Ramadan for distribution to the poor. The family allows certain poor families to graze their animals on their property. These families are specifically tied to the Elloumis, and praise their generosity whenever possible. Other poor neighbors complain of being castigated for allowing their chickens to wander on the Hajj's property. One young man who supported his parents and siblings received gifts of clothes, money, and temporary work. The Elloumis set aside a portion of wheat and other products during the harvest as part of their zakat. Still, their attitude toward the poor could be contemptuous at times:

> The lives of the poor are disorganized. They live with nature, not with their heads. The poor are the miserable in spirit. They don't respect laws. They're sneaky and will steal. They do things against religion.

Hajj Elloumi's brother is one of the town's ʿumad. He also inherited 150 hectares of land from his father. I was greeted in his personal office (not the office he kept as an ʿumda), which appeared to be a two-bedroom apartment next to his large home. A satellite dish beamed in French television. The ʿumda is a heavy-set man who chain-smokes and laughs easily. A degree of rivalry exists between him and his brother. Although his brother had received eight hundred hectares of former cooperative land, he was one of only two informants in any income group who stated a preference for cooperatives: "Cooperatives are better than privatization. Why should one person get eight hundred hectares and the next person nothing?" When asked how his family arrived at its wealth, he answered, "We were always rich."

As well as cooperatives, the ʿumda complained about the rising costs of agricultural materials. "Prices of materials have gone up. Expenses for everything are up 150 percent." He acknowledged that his fruit trees allowed him to grow a crop for export, and planned to begin cultivating more vegetables.

The ʿumda lives largely in a nuclear family framework. He does contribute the zakat, and some extra gifts to his agricultural workers. His attitude toward the poor was familiar: "The workers want villas and cars. There's a lack of sincerity with them."

A young man of thirty, Husain, was one of the most impressive members of the community. He inherited ten hectares of irrigated land from his father. In a relatively short period he bought twenty more hectares and installed expensive motorized pumps to tap into underground water. His vegetables and fruit trees have been a great success, earning more than 100,000 dinars a year in profit. Husain explained that the délégué and other administrators very quickly build relationships with successful people. Husain sees this as a natural part of the networking and relationship-building that help a young man get ahead; he has already used his administrative contacts to complete projects. He missed out on contracts for cooperatives, he said, because he was not big enough yet in town. From his point of view, those contracts went to the richest people who had built up the greatest number of contacts.

He somewhat resented the low cost of renting state lands, but this understandably did not dramatically dampen the spirit of a young man enjoying great financial success. He has a sterling reputation in town for buying land and improving production. In general Husain favors privatization, because private management is more careful and productive, yet he scoffs at any notion that the land distribution was based on economic efficiency. According to him, large farmers are driving those with two or three hectares right out of farming; they cannot compete.

Husain has become a man of power who could become a traditional patron.

He claims to make sure that anyone who has worked for him who is really struggling gets gifts during the harvest and a regular supply of vegetables. In addition, I saw myself that he gives vegetables to his two sisters' families. Their husbands are unemployed.

One of my more interesting encounters was with the lessee of a 265-hectare irrigated holding, on which grew primarily pears, apples, and grapes. Abdelkader is perhaps the town's wealthiest resident, and is a personal friend of the minister of agriculture. He controls over a thousand hectares of land in Tebourba and several hundred hectares more in nearby areas. Descended from Andalusians, the family has had large holdings and strong government contacts since the time of the beys.

My efforts to interview Abdelkader were met by stalling by several of the household's servants and by an interrogation by the man himself. I was sent to the family's lawyer, who also ran a tourism agency for the family in Tunis. The lawyer emphasized the improvement in techniques and production under private management, noting that anyone fired had been a poor employee. He claimed that his client participated through the délégué in many community welfare efforts, but looked forward to the day when his taxes and the taxes of others would be enough to handle welfare on a bureaucratic level. I was shown files of taxes paid.

A local controversy surrounded this well-placed farmer. Apparently he received a US$280,000 loan along with the cooperative contract. Much of this money was used to install the latest in refrigeration for his fruit harvests. This put him in a strong competitive position, permitting him to sell the fruit off-season. Smaller-scale farmers, especially, were put at a disadvantage. A group of these farmers went to the délégué to propose a service cooperative that would provide refrigeration for the participants. This proposal was discussed in administrative circles before Abdelkader and a few friends pressured the délégué to kill it. Shortly thereafter, it was dropped from the agenda.

Ali is another medium- to large-scale farmer whose revenue places him among the well-off. His family owns thirty-five irrigated hectares, which they devote to fruit trees, vegetables, and wheat. In addition, he owns thirty-five cows, which produce milk for the Tunis market. Ten full-time workers work on the farm. Members of his family have been significant local landowners for generations. He and his brother run the family holdings, which have declined over the years because they cannot compete with some of the large-scale farmers. The families of the two brothers pool their resources and support their parents. Ali is thirty-two years old. He deeply resents the privileged status of the wealthiest, best-connected farmers. In addition to having privileged access to land, wealthy farmers can use their access to credit to more easily shift productive activities in the most lucrative direction:

> Development of agriculture in Tunisia seems to be for the rich only. The largest, best-known farmers got more land and money from the state. They used their connections and now they control prices. The middlemen who buy our products, especially fruit, prefer the larger farmers with the biggest names. They can guarantee them quantity and future sales when they need them. This is true even in off-season, because they are using government loans to buy refrigerators. They dominate quantity, availability, and prices, so they can run us out of the market. They can afford to sell really low at times, and save some of their crop in the refrigerators. We have no choice about when we sell fruits and vegetables because we have to sell before they spoil. Later, when we have nothing left to offer, they raise their prices and make a huge profit. By that time, I've sold what I have at a loss. For example, I grow two hundred tons of apples in a year. I pay my workers, irrigation, transportation, and buy 150 boxes to put the apples in, in addition to paying taxes. One hundred and eighty of the tons have to be sold at a low price, even too low to cover expenses. Only one tenth of my crop is ever sold at a good price. In the future there will only be the very rich and the very poor. The state is making rich people and poor people only; nobody will be in the middle.
>
> Most large farmers give to their workers, both full and seasonal, in order to get higher production and popularity. Something is usually given for the zakat, and during holidays. A gift of at least forty or fifty dinars on holidays is expected of us. Also, this is the route that many poor people use to get their cooking oil for use during the year.
>
> [According to Ali, political action by the less powerful is difficult through formal channels.] You need five hundred to a thousand hectares to be in the farmers' union. The rich control everything. For example, 260 people got together and suggested a service cooperative for refrigeration. Ten or so people have refrigeration and they rent the use of it at ridiculously high prices. The service cooperative suggestion was refused because these powerful farmers would never allow that kind of competition.

Among the most lucrative land to be transferred were extensive vineyards that supplied a formerly French winery, and the surrounding olive groves. The farm still produces wine, now under the Tunisian label of *vin de Tebourba*. The French-built church on top of a mountain, though gutted and used primarily as a hideout in children's games, is still a striking local feature. In March 1991 this cooperative was offered for lease, and once again the contract went to the wealthiest, largest landowner in the area. Here, too, agricultural workers complained about cuts in labor days and numbers of permanent workers.

I spoke with a top-level employee, who revealed some information about the cooperative before the new "owner" arrived and testily ended further inquiry. I did, however, manage to see files documenting US$8000 in agricultural products and money given directly to the poor in 1993.

Two brothers in their forties from a wealthy family run a farm of more than 150 hectares. They did not lease any land from failing cooperatives, but strongly support the program. Two of their relatives received contracts, but the brothers did not appear to feel any animosity toward them. They live in very large homes adjacent to the farms, and appeared to be relaxed about their wealth. They cooperate in the production and distribution of their resources. They have owned land for generations and have investments in other industries. According to one of the brothers, a few rich families, five or six, or perhaps a few more now, dominate the town. In his view, it was good that those farmers got the land because that prevented new competition and kept social order. As I indicated in chapter 1, he claimed that the rich upheld their obligations to the poor:

> Large farmers give potatoes in every harvest; first to relatives and neighbors and then to the poor. The ʿumda gathers the potatoes from the rich and hands them out. Each family receives a hundred kilos of potatoes, and then sells some of them. Clothes and money can be given through the ʿumda or directly on holidays. However, most of these people don't deserve it. The poor come to us for the zakat or aid, but they don't come to work. We can't find people to work with olives because the work is too hard. They want comfort or they want assistance without work. If they come to the house we help the elderly but not the young.
>
> In general there is moral decay here. We have thefts and even murder. Many people cause problems in the street. Even the rich are getting spoiled. They are not doing their job of presenting new projects to society.

The final person to share his views in this income group is married to the head of the farmers' union, which had gone a year without a meeting. Tahar and his wife own around twenty hectares of irrigated land and an unknown amount that is not irrigated. They operate from the nuclear family. The land was the inheritance of Tahar's wife, who admirably learned to run it on her own; the couple now do so together. There are three dwellings on their property, one of which is very large, and they own at least two non-farm automobiles. Tahar pointed out that privatizing cooperatives would lessen stable employment and increase seasonal labor. Still, better production, for him, made it worthwhile.

According to him, small farmers should not get more land, because they do not have the resources to work it. He considers the four or five large-scale farmers "the base of society. This community will be destroyed when they die." He used communal language: "When someone is hired, he is not considered a worker. He is a part of the family. Aid is given without being asked." His view of the financial condition of agricultural workers and the poor took a striking turn once the subject of paying them came up:

> We are always looking for laborers. Most people don't want to do the hardest work that we need, like pruning the olive trees. Farmers go out looking for laborers. The laborers are in a better position than the rest of us. They all have a lot of children and use them to make a fortune. For example, a man has ten sons and they all work for four dinars a day. With ten children that's forty dinars. Laborers have villas, houses, cars. The father works; the sons work; in all, they make more than their employers. After we pay for laborers there is very little money left. No large farmers have savings accounts; all is spent on expenses. The largest farmers have land and cows but no money. Even with these troubles we have to put something aside something for the poor and something extra on holidays to keep our workers. We're the true poor.

In sum, the privatization of land and other market reforms are significantly reinforcing the domination of Tebourba by a handful of rural notables, whom several well-off people and administrators claim to be the base of their society. As these notables see the situation, they employ laborers, help the poor, offer new projects to the country, and, as leaders of local religious rituals and exchange, hold the community together.

These five or so older families and a few wealthy newcomers each have holdings of several hundred hectares. They are the ones who have assumed control of the cooperatives in the area. This is clearly a case of neo-traditionalism, since there is no reason to think that these families would have been able to once again so thoroughly dominate this region without being the beneficiaries of state agricultural policies. The younger medium-scale farmers, included here because of their high incomes, would have been the more natural leaders in a market-oriented environment, since they have demonstrated competitiveness and success.

One of these wealthy farmers argued that welfare mechanisms should be strictly bureaucratic rather than religious, though most acknowledged an obligation to help the poor with aid in various forms. The ties between the wealthy and the poor are still rarely market-related, single-stranded contracts. They are often more elaborate social exchanges, and the general impression is that the wealthy of Tebourba still promote their social standing with generosity during Islamic holidays and at other times. Even when this is not the case, they are concerned about their reputations. The recent boosts in the fortunes of this group have largely come as part of state and therefore party largess. State agents and the wealthy are thus linked, and state agents can contribute more effectively to traditional welfare mechanisms.

State agents are attempting to lessen social discontent while they pursue policies that reduce access to land and employment for poor and middle-income groups. They receive resources from the rich and distribute them at the times and in the manner generally prescribed by Islam. This has not, however, prevented the wealthy from characterizing the poor as undeserving of aid. Given the attitudes expressed here, however, state persuasion probably has prevented many more of the rich from abandoning traditional obligations. Also, by maintaining traditional links and social controls between rich and poor, state agents are promoting traditional patterns of allocating resources that are nothing like the mechanisms of the market discussed in World Bank circles.

Social action in this group is also frequently based on the extended family, since many farming operations are operated by brothers and their families. In these cases, the family budgets are more joined than separate. Diffuse patron-client ties exist, but usually between distant relatives.

A few wealthy people who missed out on the cooperative contracts criticized the program as being unfair to the less well off. Most, however, shrugged and said that large landowners are the most capable. The wealthy farmers with medium-sized holdings emphasized the obvious: recent agricultural policies are for the benefit of the rich, the old, and the best-connected. The policies have permitted a handful of traditional rural notables to once again dominate the community.

The Middle Peasants

Middle peasants tend to react to land privatization and other reforms by responding to the needs of their extended family members most hurt by the reforms. They point out how they are being forced by social obligations to carry excess labor on their farms. In addition, they make known their belief that state policy is hindering their entrepreneurial ambitions.

For the most part, middle peasants own five or fewer hectares of land, which they cultivate with family labor. Other people with much the same income may be laborers with specialized or supervisory positions. One of their biggest complaints is the lack of titles to their holdings. This is a major problem in Tunisia that the government has not been able to address even during the era of structural adjustment. Two other major concerns of the middle peasants are the fragmentation of small holdings due to inheritance and their inability to compete with larger landowners who have obtained the lion's share of government support.

Middle peasants live on their farms, which can be next to the town center or up to a few miles outside of town. Hadi worked in Libya for several years before returning to purchase five hectares of land. At thirty-seven, he has been successful so far. He irrigated the holding with part of his savings and has a healthy income. Two of his brothers work for him and he is their sole source of revenue. He refers to them as unemployed.

Hadi's view of social relationships in Tebourba has a cynical bent. He agrees that the community is defined by elaborate social relationships and exchanges of various resources, including the deference that the poor give to the rich who give the zakat, harvest gifts, and other forms of aid. According to him, the zakat is commonly given, but frequently used by the well-off to build ties with the administrators:

> Ninety percent of the wealthy give one-tenth of their products as a zakat, but they give more to the rich than to the poor. They will give to people who are doing well, especially those working for the state. People who have jobs drive by in their cars during the harvest and get kilos of everything. They do this to make connections. The state gets you ahead around here, just look at the cooperatives; the rich divided them among themselves. The state prefers the large farmers in everything. The rich get their phosphate faster. When I go in for the phosphate distributed by the state, I only get a small part. Wealthy farmers get all they need right away. You have to be a name: Hicham, Naouar, Abdelkader.

Ali, a seventy-year-old man, inherited five hectares of land. Like most others, he preferred private to cooperative ownership but resented the favoritism shown to large landowners and the fact that the change meant loss of employment for some:

> If you own something you work it better; everybody wants their own land. You tell me why the rich got the land. It went to large farmers with money. All the poor wanted was a little piece of property. All large farmers got their share. They divided the land among themselves. Some of the poor returned to their homes if they were not from around here. This isn't a good place to find work anymore. When they first divided up the cooperatives a couple of years ago there were a lot of problems, because the workers thought the land belonged

to them or their families a long time ago. The government handled those problems. The program is good, but only if you can give jobs to people.

Ali believes that the rich are less likely to help the poor than they were a generation back, partly because of the increasing role played by the state in giving things such as flour, oil, books, and clothes. He agreed that frequently state agents received these items from the local wealthy and claimed that a large number of poor people still rely on aid to survive in Tebourba:

> The naked take clothes from the dead in Tebourba like everywhere else. [Although the bonds between rich and poor are fraying, he sees no decline in extended family links.] A brother is obligated to help a brother. It is unthinkable not to. The same with children. I have four sons and they will stay with me, with their families until they get on their feet. It is hard for them now, but things will get better.

At sixty-one, Ahmad owns six hectares of irrigated land. He is expressive, wiry, and independent, demanding that I turn on the tape recorder when he criticizes government policies. We met in his fields, and our conversation was interrupted from time to time as he stopped to hunt a rabbit that he hoped to have for dinner. He obtained most of his holdings by selling used clothes for nearly a decade until he had enough money to purchase the land next to the one hectare he inherited from his father. "I sold ripped clothes in the winter," he told me, "and with patience, I bought land. I'm not like this one," and he pointed to the wealthy farmer who introduced us, "who got everything from daddy, or like the ones that the government gives everything to."

According to Ahmad, the government only helps the rich: "When I applied for access to some of the leased cooperative land my name was erased from the list, as if it were a joke." His six children work for him, and also look for work in areas other than farming. He feels an obligation to support them regardless of their age or marital status.

Taher, Ahmad's neighbor, owns seven hectares of land and a few cows, having inherited the bulk of both. He employs a few workers on a temporary basis. He is not married nor does he coordinate his activities with his extended family. In spite of his apparent independence, he says he must maintain relationships in town in order to carry on his day-to-day affairs:

> If I need a simple piece of paper, if I am competing for land or phosphate, or medicine for my cows, I need the administration. Everyone needs someone to lean on. Before I do anything, I think really hard about the best way to do it.

Usually this means relying on a contact that someone has in my family. We are connected from here to Tunis. Everyone tries to do that. You do a favor for them, and they do a favor for you. It's harder if you're poor; the poor look up to the rich like someone down deep in a grave looking up to someone in the sky. They beg and shuffle to get a little bit of something to get by on.

Husain is a supervisory technician responsible for fifteen hectares of land largely devoted to grapes. He is forty-five and has a vocational degree in agriculture. He makes a good salary but is the primary support of his two sisters and his mother as well as his wife and children, which frequently puts him in a bind. He views government policies and local institutions as basically serving only the rich:

> I tried to join the farmers' union, but they refused my application because I didn't have any land. I wanted to join precisely because I wanted their help to get some land. The government had a program to give land to agricultural technicians. I had my diploma, but they said that I was too old. You have to be under forty years old and I was forty-two. I think this is unfair because I know more than younger men. They were only giving the technicians a little part of all the thousands and thousands of hectares that they were giving the large landowners. Still, that's why the farmers' union wouldn't help me; they wanted the small part given to technicians! Around here the wealthy wanted all the land, and they got it. Some have one hundred or two hundred hectares and they wanted one to two hundred more. Small farmers with two to five hectares got nothing, and they are too weak to do anything about it.

ᶜAli owns fifteen to twenty hectares of non-irrigated land on the side of a mountain. He grows olives primarily. The land had been part of a cooperative that was privatized in 1970, and ᶜAli received it because he had worked on the cooperative. His family also raises livestock and is beginning to grow grapes. ᶜAli complains that the state doesn't do anything to help small farmers, and sees the farmers' union as a waste of time for anyone but the very rich. Some people at the low end of the revenue scale, according to him, are growing desperate.

> Something like two hectares of land is not enough for a large family. I don't understand why the government sees this, and yet keeps giving land to the rich. It wasn't like this during the cooperatives with Ben Salah, and it wasn't like this in the 1970s. But that is the way it is now. The people today don't understand the economy. Nouria knew what to do. He stood the country on its feet after Ben Salah destroyed it. People were ripping olive trees out of the ground on the sides of all of these mountains and selling their livestock for virtually nothing to avoid cooperatives that they knew would be a disaster. Nouira saved the economy, but he did not help only the rich. A good economy

means that every family has enough to provide for themselves and their country. Nouira understood this.

ᶜAli pointed out that mutual aid is common in Tebourba because usually it is a matter of blood relationships and Islam, which requires that some aid be given to the poor. The poor still make the rounds during the harvest, so that the custom of people helping each other out continues. One of his three sons and his wife and daughter live and work with him. The other two sons have families and their own household budgets.

Bourthia is a widow of fifty-five. She owns ten hectares of land, which her next-door neighbor cultivates for her with the aid of his sons. She has noticed that unemployment has increased under economic reform: "many people have lost their jobs because of the privatization program." She prefers the cooperatives for the workers' sake. She shares a general community hostility toward ownership of land in Tebourba by those from outside. "The land is for the people of Tebourba; outsiders come in and take your bread." Her general view of the rich is captured in a proverb: "Money makes the ass the head." Still, she thinks that many of the wealthy give aid to the poor because they fear social criticism.

Hadi owns six hectares of irrigated land, where he grows primarily artichokes. He had been a merchant and bought this holding in 1970, when a former cooperative worker was unable to pay for the materials to cultivate land he had been granted by the state. Over the years he has invested in a well, and improved the land in other ways. He, his wife, and five children do most of the agricultural labor. On occasion he hires temporary labor. Hadi deals primarily with his nuclear family, and his resources are not strained by the demands of extended family members. In a familiar complaint, he agreed with the wisdom of market reforms, but resented the fact that the benefits have not been shared:

> The problem with privatization is that one person gets the land. The land should be spread out. All of us can profit. If it's a large lot two or three people should get it. The state should choose from the people who specialize in farming. With small farmers six to ten hectares is enough, because they do not have the credit to handle more. One awful thing should be avoided: in some areas journalists and lawyers are getting state land. They use laborers who don't know farming.

Husain, a man of sixty-three, was one of the most pleasant people one can meet. We sat in his field of pear trees while he made tea on a small charcoal bed. He was concerned about the lack of a deed to his five-hectare irrigated

farm, the state's seeming disdain for small-scale farmers, and the inadequacy
of the help provided by the rich:

> The workers on state farms had salaries and retirement funds; with the new
> program they had to find other work without benefits. The well-connected
> wealthy are getting the land. The small farmers are waiting for the state com-
> mittees to do something about their conditions. We are still waiting for deeds.
> I'm scared that they will take my farm. I have eight children living with me;
> six are married with children of their own. The rich are being given fertilizer
> by the state. In order to participate in this you need papers that most of us
> don't have, and even if you do they tell you that you don't produce enough
> products to deserve fertilizer. Small farmers can't get loans from anybody but
> their family. Many small farmers sold their land because we can't compete.
> They went to Tunis and most of them are doing worse now. It doesn't make
> sense for the country. Large farmers overwork people and don't hire enough
> people.
> Connections dominate these things, and if you want a job, it is purely about
> connections. Diplomas are irrelevant. Poor people don't have connections. In
> April I needed some medication, but they told me that it would take two
> months. I was so sick that I couldn't eat. I told my cousin who knew someone
> and we got it in seven days. These things can mean life or death.
> The wealthy have nothing to worry about around here. They bond and work
> together. It doesn't matter if they are from Teboura or not. Big families here
> bond with outsider big families, and the state looks after all of them. Many of
> them can be good with workers: they give them things during festivals and
> they can afford bonuses during the harvest.

Tuhami owns three hectares of land watered by a well. The land was bought
by his father, who had recently passed away when I spoke with him. He has five
brothers who work with him, cultivating vegetables, fruit trees, and olives. In
addition to farming with his brothers, he supplies vegetables to cousins, aunts,
and uncles. Tuhami and his brothers are committed to the market, but dislike
the state's favoritism for large farmers. The experience of cooperatives has left
them with a derisive attitude toward Ben Salah and socialism. "Ben Salah is
known to have said, if someone has five dinars, either I gave it to them or they
stole it." The general views of privatization among this socioeconomic group
reflected a preference for market reforms aimed at encouraging all income
groups to participate:

> There is more production with private ownership, but there were only oppor-
> tunities for large landowners. No information was given to anyone else. Small
> farmers are losing hope around here. It was already hard to compete. In terms

of workers, there was no clear understanding of new ownership. Most workers were opposed, but they didn't react because they feared the new relationship between the new owners and the state. They were scared of being fired and afraid to go against a state project. A lot of them were fired anyway.

Habib owns ten hectares of irrigated land. The parcel was an inheritance. He employs people (usually his cousins) to cultivate the apples and vegetables on his farm, while educating his four children for other work. Habib views private ownership as vastly superior to cooperatives because individuals who care work harder than people working for the state. (The comment reflects how far away cooperatives in Tunisia were from worker ownership.) He resented the fact that land went to those with money and connections, stating that he tried to get a group of family members together to invest in a project, but the state preferred individual owners with resources.

People with fewer resources have to deal with the situation:

> The new owners use fewer workers, but what can people do? Some leave Tebourba. Some did nothing and now their families support them. A few of them had a bit of land that they are trying to live on. People help the poor around here. Even today at the harvest one-tenth is given to the poor. The rich will take care of the poor during catastrophes, weddings, festivals, and funerals. The rich don't allow the poor to get rich or starve. The owners have to know the poor and help them from time to time in order to have good workers during the harvest. It would help here if there was leveling of wealth. That's my hope. There are too many poor people to have others running around with Mercedeses, trucks, satellite dishes, and twenty color televisions.
>   . . . I am the main breadwinner for my family and my mother. During ceremonies I give to the poor and my relatives. My cousins depend on me for money and I provide them with work.

In general, the middle peasants are feeling squeezed by agricultural policies that favor the rich. The poorer ones are being run out of farming, while better-off middle peasants have a harder time competing with farmers who can use their control of supply and refrigeration to manipulate prices and middlemen. Wealthier farmers also have better access to credit and agricultural materials. Smallholders' lack of secure titles is also a serious problem. The state has made feeble efforts to deal with these issues.

Nuclear family members usually provide the labor force, while brothers and cousins who are struggling are included when calculating the production and distribution of resources. Relatives in need can also expect gifts of vegetables to bolster their food supply. There is great sympathy among the middle peasants for cooperative workers fired during the recent privatization efforts. Along with agricultural laborers, these former workers wait for the state to make a concerted effort to deal with their concerns. The comments of the informants suggest that they are feeling like an abandoned constituency.

Access to Formal Institutions

Norman Uphoff and Milton Esman note that farmers' associations in developing countries tend to become the tools of wealthier farmers, while poorer ones are left out in the cold or forced to rely on traditional patron-client relations. "If such organizations became institutionalized, they would be instruments of the large and middle farmers, while smaller farmers would be thrown back on traditional links of dependency on patrons or be compelled to rely wholly on their own meager resources" (Uphoff and Esman 1974, 66). This pattern largely appears in rural Tunisia; and other trends in formal institutions appear to be increasingly favoring the strong over the weak.

Wealthy farmers of Tebourba appear to be exercising their political power by not allowing the farmers' union to meet in recent years, thereby preventing small-scale farmers from voicing displeasure with agricultural policies. When queried, large-scale farmers said that the union did not have a place to meet. Poorer farmers claimed that the wealthy had many ways to keep them out of the union, including a farm size requirement; and at any rate the farmers' union was simply a tool for the rich to help themselves, so there was no reason to attend. These circumstances vary from the situation described by Mira Zussman in her earlier study of Tebourba. At that time the union met regularly and it had four functions:

> First and foremost—and in contrast to European and American unions—it is a forum for communication of Ministry of Agriculture objectives. Second, it is a meeting place for the small group of Tebourba's wealthy landowners. Third, it is a place of articulating problems and mobilizing farmers. And fourth, it is a place where poor farmers come to make contact with the wealthy—particularly when they need a favor. (Zussman 1992, 101–102)

Many segments of Tebourban society would like to change recent agricultural policies, yet the farmers' union did not meet once in the year of this study. I was informed that it had been several years since poor farmers had even bothered to attend the union's meetings.

Large farmers and local officials, often the same people, have exercised their power to limit the formal participation of poor peasants in other areas of the country as well. Some of the handicaps faced by small farmers as they attempt to enter a market economy were documented by Richard Fraenkel and Mathew Shane in their study of Ebba Ksour in northern Tunisia:

> Through elective office large farmers enjoy greater power in such participatory institutions as the local mutual credit union. Another restraint on small farmer access to the services of public institutions is the requirement that all applications for their services must be approved by the local officials of the Ministry of Agriculture. The Ministry of the Interior is the most important organization determining the distribution of purchased resources for cereals production. . . . The shaykh or omda, the lowest official of the Ministry of the Interior, is responsible for a territorial sub-unit of a delegation. The shaykh's approval is needed for applications made by farmers to be sent to the appropriate branch of a technical ministry.
>
> The shaykhs were recruited from among the local population. All of the shaykhs in the locality studied were large farmers who rented a high percentage of the land they operated from small farmers. Small farmers complained frequently of refusals by the shaykhs to accept their applications for institutional services.
>
> After the reversal of the collectivization program, the government recognized the need of helping the private cereals producers to start-up production. Two policies were decided. . . . The first was to make loans available to small farmers from the mutual credit union system. The second was to liberalize machinery credit policy. But, as we shall see, these policies did not permit the small farmer as an operator.
>
> . . . An examination of the amounts of loans made by the credit union after 1969 to small farmers showed that these were in fact consumption subsidies; it would not have been possible to start-up cereals production even using the traditional technology with loans which were as small as 9 dinars. . . . A second problem is the relative power of large and small farmers in the credit union of Ebba-Ksour. Lending decisions are made by the union's board, all of whose eight members are large farmers in the locality. . . . This is not in itself evidence that small farmers do not get loans from the credit union, but examination of a list of loan recipients from 1970 to 1973 showed it to be generally true. (Fraenkel and Shane 1974, 25–28)

Fraenkel and Shane concluded that market conditions kept most small farmers in the traditional agricultural sector after they left cooperatives. Some rented their land to large landowners, who could obtain the credit to mechanize

and to use high-yield seed varieties. Most of the dividends of modern technology went to large landowners. Small farmers' rental arrangements and the
grazing terms for their livestock kept them tied to large farmers.

Summary

Nicholas Hopkins (1983) defined a moral economy as a type of social organization in which the poor are enmeshed in a system of social controls that
ties them to the rich. This is an apt description of Tebourba today, if one adds
that the system of social controls also ties the poor to the state via bureaucratic
and traditional welfare mechanisms. The striking feature of social arrangements in this community is the extent to which state agents act to maintain
traditional social controls linking poor to rich. The délégué and the ʿumad
make their rounds of the wealthy to insure that substantial redistribution will
occur during the harvest and Islamic festivals.

It is apparent that the wealthy would not have maintained traditional welfare mechanisms to the degree that they have without the prodding of party
officials and the bureaucratic establishment (who incidentally could point to
benefits of state policy as leverage). The wealthy could have used the official
state ideology of economic liberalism to justify abandoning their traditional
obligations to the poor. Economic changes have allowed them to increase
mechanization and lessened their need for labor, cheap or otherwise.

Local government officials have another agenda. They are responsible to
their superiors for maintenance of political and social stability at a time when
government policies mean setbacks for some, and outright destitution for others. It is interesting that these officials, who are members of a government
strongly committed to economic liberalism, are willing to turn to the traditional system of social controls based on Islamic welfare mechanisms in order
to keep down the social and political resistance of the poor. If these mechanisms fail to prevent conflagrations, outright repression might follow. At any
rate, the redistributive mechanisms allocate community resources in the in-
efficient ways that market reforms are designed to remedy. Invigoration of
these mechanisms by state agents and their wealthy allies can only serve to dis-
tance community social action from the market-oriented behavior theoretically promoted by state-led economic liberalization.

We should also note here that state agents are reinforcing traditional social
arrangements based on Islam. The Islamic nature of these welfare mechanisms
make them a logical fallback for all income groups, even in circumstances that

give freer rein to self-interest. This adds a wrinkle to the possibility of false consciousness leading the poor to accept the social arrangements desired by the wealthy and powerful. Poor people, just like anyone else, are largely aware of maneuvers by people that harm their interests. They also calculate their behavior and public utterances in various ways to promote their interests in a field of power that offers them limited options. However, some poor people are truly religious, and may internalize Islam-based social arrangements and resource distribution simply because they are Muslims. The same can be said for wealthy Muslims aware of the need to purify wealth through almsgiving.

Inadvertently, however, the state may be reinforcing political identification based primarily on Islam, regardless of whether subsequent groupings are based on class or on other identities. The distribution of aid according to an Islamic hierarchy cannot help but provide conceptual support for the Islamist opposition. Like al-Nahda, the state gives Islamic traditions a prominent role in the distribution of resources. From there it is natural to consider Islam as a source for broader political organization as well.

Poor residents of Tebourba face their increasing hardship by turning to the most reliable of traditional peasant institutions—blood kinship. The extended family becomes active during crises and, contrary to rational actor arguments, appears to be the primary level of solidarity and guarantee of subsistence. In hard times or not, the strength and flexibility of poor rural dwellers is evident here. Donor agencies and government officials underline the capacity of the rural poor to increase their income through self-employment, private monetary transfers from city workers to relatives in rural areas, and temporary low-paying jobs. They stress this in spite of increasing unemployment, especially in cities, and a pitiful level of direct support from a government that provides support in abundance to their wealthy counterparts.

Middle peasants, especially the better-off ones, are somewhat bemused by government policies that favor the largest landowners. The rent on state lands is far below market value and the credit that flows to renters of cooperative lands can be used in various ways to gain advantage in the market. Still, many of these smaller farmers are dynamic and productive. They have been cited by outside observers as the group with the best potential to increase agricultural production and efficiency. Middle peasants also have been the ones to respond to their relatives in need. Their farms are becoming crowded with the surplus labor of unemployed relatives.

The distribution of cooperatives in Tebourba to large landowners seems anachronistic. It has primarily benefited rural notables with large landholdings, sometimes granted in beylical concessions. The names of Elloumi, Toumi, and others of Andalusian descent have gained even more in prominence. On the other hand, the descendants of the squatters, today's small peasantry, have had to realize that the fact that they and their ancestors lived their lives on Tebourba's land was ultimately not enough to secure a claim on it.

In sum, social organization in Tebourba retains a surprising level of traditional patterns in spite of state-led economic liberalization. This is not to say that individualistic wealth-maximizing behavior is uncommon. It is to assert that political behavior in Tebourba today, during economic liberalization, is better understood by recognizing complex forms of social exchange than by beginning with self-interested, individualistic behavior.

This interpretation of rural social organization differs from a class analysis that focuses on a conflict evolving between agricultural laborers and landowners. The presence of numerous small-scale family farms impedes such a development. Also, patron-client ties and other traditional peasant institutions are linking poor and rich in ways that limit direct conflict, and the concentration of resources in the hands of the wealthy in Tebourba has been accompanied by increasing mechanization, which limits the need for labor and forces many agricultural laborers to leave the area altogether.

A rational actor approach suggests that there would be many individuals among the poor, middle, and wealthy peasants ready and able to ignore traditional obligations and exploit the opportunities of increasing marketization. Traditional community institutions would be a smaller part of the story of social action. Members of all income groups would have a better chance to thrive in a more market-oriented economy.

Some moral economy approaches focus on village-level institutions and do not see how central the solidarity of the extended family is in guaranteeing subsistence. These approaches also tend not to focus on the role of the state in maintaining traditional peasant institutions. In *Weapons of the Weak* (1985), James Scott noted the decline of a moral economy in rural Malaysia during the green revolution without a serious effort by state agents to maintain the social controls that are embedded in a moral economy.

My interpretation agrees with analysts seeking approaches to human behavior that acknowledge the capacity of people to utilize more than one form of social action at a time. It is in accord with people who doubt that one can make economic generalizations about poor and rich cultivators, and it therefore analyzes different income groups separately.

What I am saying here falls in line somewhat with Theda Skocpol's central proposition that the state structures social life (Skocpol 1979). In a North African application of this approach, Lisa Anderson (1986) has pointed out the role of the state in maintaining traditional patronage relations in rural Tunisia. My more recent work seeks to heighten awareness of how and to what extent state agents have structured social organization in rural communities of Tunisia during the process of economic reform.

Finally, this analysis provides a local or microlevel view of how economic reform facilitated a transition to a less populist form of authoritarianism. Like developments in the national political economy, neo-liberal reforms and the strategies political elites have used to manage constituencies combine to reinforce the dominance of economic elites. During both ISI populism and the new market era, corporatism in urban areas and clientelism in the countryside remain the most potent state strategies to control the mass of their populations.

An agricultural laborer.

Wheat fields of a wealthy
farmer.

A middle peasant and the author, kneeling.

Tebourba horizon.

❖ 5 ❖

STRUCTURAL ADJUSTMENT AND
THE SMALL PEASANTRY

NEO-LIBERAL REFORMS sponsored by the World Bank and the IMF can have various effects on the political and social structure of the receiving nation. The impact of these reforms can perhaps best be discerned at the sector or even community level. As the last chapter demonstrated, these reforms may serve to entrench a status quo unfavorable to the poor, they may make the situation considerably worse, or they may undermine that situation and help the poor become more important participants in the new market arrangements the reforms seek to create.

Conventional structural adjustment theory locates the greatest equity gains from economic reform in the countryside. This chapter uses the cases of Tunisia and other developing countries to challenge this view. Several factors contribute to growing inequalities within rural areas during agricultural economic liberalization. Land policies frequently increase the disparity of asset distribution. Broader agricultural policies fail to sufficiently integrate the landless and land-poor into export-led growth. Economic and political power figure strongly in the resolution of conflicts created by new tenure and other market arrangements. National government officials and local bureaucrats implementing neo-liberal reforms may place political considerations and rent-seeking opportunities ahead of economic efficiency and equity. Women are often disadvantaged in structural adjustment programs. Truly representative farmers' organizations and other parts of civil society rarely participate in the process of determining economic reform policy, which transforms the lives of rural dwellers. Taken together, in many countries, these factors culminate in market economic changes that favor rural elites, increase rural asset disparities, and make no serious efforts to alleviate rural poverty. The World Bank is well aware of these potential pitfalls in neo-liberal market reforms, and it produces studies to address them. However, there is a gap between rhetoric and practice in World Bank policy that permits the institution to financially support states determined to (re-)concentrate rural economic and political power.

Equity and Structural Adjustment

Theoretically, neo-liberal reforms improve the material circumstances of most rural dwellers. Broad material improvements in the countryside should occur because the reforms increase the value of tradeables relative to non-tradeables, and in developing countries the agricultural sector is generally the principal producer of tradeables:

> The analytical core of conventional adjustment theory turns on the combination of expenditure reduction and expenditure switching resulting from a real devaluation. In the latter case . . . the price of tradeables rises relative to that of nontradeables. . . . The expenditure switching process clearly attracts considerable significance for the agricultural sector. . . . This is because in most developing countries, agriculture is the principal source of tradeables output. Furthermore, when, as in many sub-Saharan countries, agricultural tradeables producers have been discriminated against through pricing, marketing and taxation rules, adjustment policies have generally sought to reverse such discriminatory practices. (Commander 1989, xii)

Other contributors to the literature on the social costs of structural adjustment more directly suggest that all groups in the agricultural sector should benefit from the reforms. "Government changes in producer prices for agricultural goods lead to demands for labor and improved wages. Thus, urban bias is reversed, and small and large landowners benefit" (Nelson 1992, 227). "Better prices for farmers and improved agrarian services [due to structural adjustment] alleviate poverty in rural areas where it is the most widespread" (Herbst 1993, 147). Herbst sees little moral or policy reason to explore the impact of structural adjustment on various income groups in rural areas:

> In fact, almost everyone in Ghana, and almost all other African countries, is poor on an objective basis. Therefore, the fact that adjustment programs may not directly benefit the absolute poorest should have far less policy and moral implications than if there were a bias in a rich country. If adjustment programs help a significant number of people in Africa, then inevitably a large number of the poor will be helped. (1993, 147)

The optimistic assessment of academics—structural adjustment decreases rural inequality and improves the circumstances of the rural poor—is echoed by World Bank officials in reports on Tunisian agricultural sector adjustment:

> (a) the rural poor, particularly in rainfed areas, will profit from increased agricultural producer prices as well as from increases in agricultural production for import substitution and exports; (b) the urban poor will profit from the increase in the minimum wage introduced in mid-1986; and (c) both groups will profit from the stimulating effects of the adjustment measures on employment creation, as export industries, agriculture, and tourism are all relatively labor-intensive sectors. (World Bank 1986a, 16)

The reasons, cited by the World Bank and academics, why structural adjustment should benefit rural dwellers of all socioeconomic groups do not apply in the Tunisian case due to inegalitarian land policies, broader sector policies that do not aid the small peasantry, and dispute resolution procedures favoring the powerful. New land policies in Tunisia have a nearly absurd bias toward large landowners. World Bank officials have noted that the unequal distribution of state land in Tunisia during structural adjustment has contributed to rural poverty:

> Allocation of state-owned and collective land to private title holders is occuring, with at best neutral, and probably negative consequences for the poor. . . . The government is expressly not distributing these lands to improve the land assets of the rural poor. (World Bank 1995b, annex C.3, 6)

The unequal distribution of land, the lack of title and land rights, and the fragmentation of land contribute to the persistence of rural poverty. Land policies could reduce poverty in two ways: by improving the security of farmers' existing rights to land and by making more land accessible to farmers. Tunisia has chosen to try to improve tenure security, but with apparently modest results.

> The ability of farmers to significantly improve their welfare on the basis of agricultural activities will continue to be severely constrained by the small size of their farms. There is some potential for increasing the access of the poor to land through the distribution of state lands, but that would require a reversal of current policy. (World Bank 1995a, 26)

The World Bank's agricultural sector loan supported the privatization of agricultural production cooperatives under the rubric of improving the management of natural resources:

Recently, the Government has begun offering some collective land to private companies (Sociétés de Mise en Valeur) and making efforts to improve the management of others through the preparation of integrated development plans supported by credit. (World Bank 1986b, 9)

Even though nothing in the guidelines dictated the transfer of land to rural notables, the fact that the cooperatives were not broken up and the reality of who has received the cooperative contracts leads to the conclusion that large landowners were meant to be the primary beneficiaries of this land privatization program.[1] The state announced three general steps in the leasing of state lands: First, a list is published in all major newspapers of production cooperatives available for leasing. An address is provided to which detailed project proposals can be submitted. Second, the administrations of the Ministries of State Land and Agriculture review the applications and consult at the local level in deciding who will win the contracts. Third, the state, with its administrative branches, supervises the renting; the administration supervises the implementation of the proposals, which in bureaucratic parlance become *Sociétés de Mise en Valeur* (improvement companies). In practice, the state landholdings are run with little if any supervision. The long-term leases (twenty-five to fifty years) were scheduled for full privatization at a later date.[2]

An important question arises from this discussion. Was Tunisian state land leased to wealthy landowners, rather than to middle peasants, smallholders, or competent laborers, because of the government's internal decisions or as a result of the World Bank's structural adjustment program? On the whole, it seems that Tunisian officials were intent on both privatizing cooperatives, which were a drain on state coffers, and strengthening bonds with their core constituency of rural notables. It also appears that government officials took advantage of donor agency and academic pronouncements that structural adjustment benefited all income groups in the agricultural sector; echoing these claims, they undertook a policy that in reality benefited their powerful allies.

The land transfer is also remarkable because large landowners in Tunisia did

---

1. Economic data in Tunisia, particularly data related to land tenure and the distribution of income, are treated like state secrets. Under supervision I was allowed to view and take notes on the regulations concerning the leasing of cooperative land, but not to copy or take away documents. My access to figures documenting production in the leased cooperatives was similarly restricted.

2. Director of the Ministry of State Lands, interviewed by the author.

not modernize or increase agricultural production during earlier agrarian reforms:

> The majority of the larger private landowners were perfectly happy to go on as before. The existing situation [traditional farming, absenteeism, leasing, living off rents] gave them no reason to be dissatisfied from a private point of view. This left the state and the cooperatives with almost the whole burden of making the necessary investment in the transformation of Tunisian agriculture. At the same time, they had to contend with the continued existence and even expansion of the larger private properties, which severely restricted the possibilities of effective action on an important portion of the land most suitable for agricultural diversification and intensification. Rural employment remained unchanged and the total agricultural production of the country showed little increase. (Liner 1970, 7)

The Tunisian government's structural adjustment program also supported the privatization of collective lands. However, because of the way tenure disputes have been resolved, this policy has resulted in major asset losses for the poor. There are 2.7 million hectares of communal lands in Tunisia, divided evenly between crop- and rangeland. The country's mid-term structural adjustment program supports policies that had been followed in the country for years prior:

> While no analysis exists on how Tunisia's rural poor have fared in the implementation of the policy of privatizing communal lands, concerns are raised that the impact may well be negative. First, the poor are least able to defend their traditional rights as communal land is subdivided, particularly since these rights may have been sporadic and partial, even if essential for their welfare. Such use rights are difficult to preserve following private titling. Second, the rural poor often use communal land as a kind of insurance policy, relying on it periodically if they face set-backs in their primary income generating activities. With privatization of communal land and reduced access by the rural poor, they lose this base of income stabilization and generation. (World Bank 1995b, annex C.3, 7)

Broader structural adjustment agricultural policies have also failed to benefit the landless and land-poor. The agricultural sector reforms aimed to improve the framework of prices and incentives, reorient the public investment program (offering subsidized credit to rural elite beneficiaries of state land privatization and, to be fair, also offering new credit programs to the rural poor midway through the reform process), strengthen basic support services for farmers, and privatize those that were economically viable. It also aimed to improve natural resource management and improve the capability of the Ministry of Agriculture to monitor and analyze (World Bank 1991a, iii).

According to World Bank studies there was almost no net job creation in agriculture during the structural adjustment period (World Bank 1995b, annex C.1, 1). The World Bank also admits that the poorest farmers have received few benefits from improved producer prices because they needed undelivered state support to take advantage of the new market opportunities:

> The agricultural price policies between 1986 and 1992 could have affected the rural poor both as asset holders and as agricultural wage earners. Although data constraints make it difficult to quantitatively assess the direct impact of these policies on the income of the rural poor, signs are that the effects are minor. As asset holders, poor rural households experienced only marginally positive income effects from the changes in agricultural trade and input subsidy policies under the reform program. Agricultural price policies reduced input subsidies and adjusted producer prices to be more in line with world markets. Except for the deep cuts in olive oil producer prices in late 1993, price policies have had a minor direct income effect on poor farmers. With little access to irrigation, the poorest farmers are affected mainly by prices for rainfed crops and livestock. Substantial cuts in subsidies for fertilizers, pesticides, animal feed, and irrigation water also had little impact on the incomes of poor farmers because of their low use of these inputs. (World Bank 1995a, 20)

The export crops favored in the new policy environment require irrigation, refrigeration, and other resources that small farmers typically lack. The prices for rainfed crops and livestock produced by the poor have actually dropped in this period (World Bank 1995b, annex C.3, 1). In the mid-1990s, poor farmers confronted a dramatic shift to their detriment in government price policy for olive oil. Prices were declining internationally, and it was difficult to find export markets. Olive oil producer prices were slashed by 40 percent in 1993. This not only erased the real price increases that producers had enjoyed since the mid-1980s, it also reduced the price to about 15 percent below the lowest real price since 1980. The impact on rural incomes is thus major, affecting not only the owners of olive trees but also the seasonal laborers whom the orchard owners no longer hire to harvest and prune (World Bank 1995b, annex C.3, 1).[3]

In sum, nothing about the Tunisian case supports the notion that the entire agricultural sector will benefit from structural adjustment programs as currently conceived and implemented. The programs' land, price, and tenure-

---

3. Olive oil prices and export markets improved somewhat in the late 1990s.

dispute policies benefited the elite, and collective organizations to protect the interests of the small peasantry were thwarted.

Farm Size and Productivity

Tunisia's structural adjustment program's failure to emphasize developing small and medium-sized farms is especially odd since Tunisian farmers are primarily small-scale and low-income. Small- and medium-scale farmers are also more dynamic and productive cultivators in Tunisia than large-scale farmers. The smaller commercialized farms implement the most diversified cropping patterns, while large farmers specialize in cereals and forage crops (Radwan, Jamal, and Ghose 1991, 38).

There is also a large body of general literature that supports focusing state agricultural policy on these producers. This analytical literature investigates the relationship between farm size and productivity. Its central theme is that smaller holdings are more productive than larger ones per unit of land. At the heart of the argument is a factual observation: small farms in developing countries tend to be more productive than large ones. This theoretical literature, accompanied by substantial empirical verification from various sources, indicates that policies aimed at better distributing rural assets should reduce poverty, lessen inequality, and contribute to economic efficiency (Lipton 1977; Berry and Cline 1979; Cassen 1994; Bardham, Bowles, and Gintis 1998).

The arguments supporting the superior productivity of smaller holdings highlight their reliance on cheaper family labor (instead of hired labor), which leads to greater productivity and a higher rate of land cultivation than on large ones. A broad result is that land goes relatively underused on large farms, while excess labor is crowded onto small farms (Berry and Cline 1979, 29). For Jensen and Meckling (1976) the fundamental reason that family-operated farms are more efficient is that large-scale operations bear the supervision costs of managing wage labor and enforcing effort. Michael Lipton's (1977) pathbreaking work *Why Poor People Stay Poor* spoke to the promise of owner-operated family farms in the development process:

> In early development, with labour plentiful and the ability to save scarce, small farming is especially promising, because it is the part of the economy in which a given amount of scarce investible resources will be supported by the most human effort. Thus it is emphasis upon small farming that can most rapidly boost income per head to the levels at which the major sacrifices of consump-

tion, required for heavy industrialization, can be undertaken without intolerable hardship and repression. (Lipton 1977, 23)

Following this theme, Berry and Cline (1979, 6–30) provide several related reasons to favor small farms in state policy. First, market imperfections, such as subsidy programs and greater access to credit for purchase of land and machinery, tend to favor large farms. Such structural advantages render the effective price of land higher for small farms than for large ones and reinforce the more extensive use of labor on small farms. Facing a higher price for capital, small farmers tend to substitute labor for equipment. As such, they better exploit labor resources and yield more output per unit of land.

Second, large uncultivated landholdings also undermine average output levels. Some elites hold stretches of property for reasons of political power, prestige, or speculative gain, and are uninterested in taking the risk of exploiting its productive potential. This land non-usage, which needless to say is rare among small family farmers, contradicts developing countries' need for agricultural productivity.

Third, large farms may at times constrain production in order to avoid flooding a local market with a certain product and so driving down prices. A small farmer is much less likely to cut output, because he will rarely be in a position to monopolize a market. Fourth, and similarly, if large farms fear overproduction it is because they are unable to make beneficial use of surpluses that cannot be sold on the market. Family farms, on the other hand, do not face this risk, because families can consume a considerable percentage of yields in the event of unfavorable prices. Hence, the danger of over-production need not inhibit land and labor utilization on small farms.

Defenders of large farms respond with several counterarguments. First, they argue that yields are actually higher on large farms. Berry and Cline reply that this is a result of the tendency of large farmers to limit cultivation to a portion of their land that is of higher quality and thus produces greater yields. This selective utilization leaves much land unexploited, and thus makes large farms less efficient in the long run.

Second, some contend that full utilization of farm machinery requires a minimum farm size. Berry and Cline (1979, 6) question the relevancy of this argument for the developing world, "where the scarcity of capital and the abundance of labor recommend against the use of costly machines." In those cases where large machinery might be useful, they add, improved rental programs could easily make it more accessible for small farmers. Jodha (1984) adds that machinery alone rarely increases optimal farm size beyond the level in which family labor is fully utilized. Lanjouw (1995) and Deininger and Binswanger (1999) found that the optimal size of a farm generally does not exceed the scale at which family labor is fully occupied (utilizing seasonal hired labor for specific tasks).

Finally, some allege that, because large farmers are better educated and more aware of change, they adopt technological innovations more quickly and dynamically than do small farmers. Berry and Cline counter this assertion with several points. First, mechanization is not necessarily equivalent to a truly dynamic employment of new techniques. Second, although large farms might be the first to adopt new technology, small farms usually follow in time. Finally, any greater dynamism among large farms is probably attributable to the market advantages that they enjoy. Berry and Cline (1979, 27) infer that "the main policy implication is that the channels for credit and modern inputs to small farms should be improved—not that a large farm structure is essential for the adoption of new techniques." This central proposition has been validated by several recent publications (Deininger and Binswanger 1999; World Bank 2000).

The Evolution of the World Bank's Land Policy

The World Bank's policy in dealing with land issues and rural poverty has, since at least the mid-1970s, supported structural reforms that redistribute land downward, not upward as has occurred in Tunisia. In 1975 the World Bank published *The Assault on World Poverty,* a document establishing that Bank policy should support rural projects that led to greater equality in rural assets, including land reform, and deny aid to those countries that did not pursue such policies. The document revealed ambitious goals for equity in the rural development process:

> 1) The World Bank will give priority in agricultural lending to those member countries that pursue broad-based agricultural strategies directed toward the promotion of adequate new employment opportunities, with special attention to the needs of the poorest groups. The Bank will support policies of land reform designed to further these objectives.

2) The Bank will make it known that it stands ready to finance special projects and programs that may be a necessary concomitant of land reform, so long as the reforms and related programs are consistent with the objectives stated in the previous paragraph. These programs would include credit, technical services and infrastructure projects designed to meet the special needs of land reform beneficiaries.

3) The Bank will cooperate with the Food and Agriculture Organization of the United Nations (FAO), the United Nations Development Programme (UNDP) and other organizations to provide support and assistance to member governments seeking help with the specification and design of land reform programs where these are in keeping with the Bank's objectives. This support will include financial and technical aid with cadastral surveys, registration and land titles and similar services.

4) The Bank will continue to explore, through its agricultural and rural development projects, ways of providing for a distribution of benefits consistent with the goals outlined under (1) above, including appropriate tenurial arrangements and projects designed to serve the needs of small farmers and settlers.

5) The Bank will intensify its effort through the sector and country economic work to identify and draw attention to the need and opportunities for land reform with respect to existing tenurial situations and their economic effects.

6) The Bank will support and encourage research related to the economics of land reform in its broadest aspects, including its social dimensions. It will continue its support for programs of economic and technical research directed toward the special needs of the type of small farmer likely to emerge from land reforms.

7) The Bank will undertake studies of the costs and benefits of settlement projects, with particular attention to developing approaches which will lower the cost per family settled.

8) The Bank will not support projects where land rights are such that a major share of the benefits will accrue to high-income groups

unless increases in output and improvements in the balance of payments are overriding considerations; in such cases, it will carefully consider whether the fiscal arrangements are appropriate to ensure that a reasonable share of the benefits accrues to the government.

9) In circumstances where increased productivity can effectively be achieved only subsequent to land reform, the Bank will not support projects which do not include land reform.

10) Where land is held under some form of tenancy, the Bank will foster the adoption of tenancy conditions and sharecropping arrangements that are equitable and conducive to the optimal use of resources.

11) Where land is communally held without regulation of access, the Bank will encourage subdivision, if sedentary forms of agriculture are possible, or pursue land usage and access arrangements that are compatible with the long-run productivity of the land and the welfare of the resident population.

12) The Bank will pay particular attention to the consequences of the interaction of the new technology and the prevailing institutional structures, as reflected in the pattern of land ownership, in order to avoid adjustments which will increase the maldistribution of income and cause economic hardship. (World Bank 1975, 201–202)

In addition to these documents, in 1975 the World Bank issued a land reform policy paper (LRPP) to directly guide its policy in this area (Deininger and Binswanger 1999). Key principles enunciated in the LRPP were the desirability of owner-operated family farms on both efficiency and equity grounds; the need to promote markets to facilitate efficiency-enhancing transfers to more efficient users; and the desirability of an egalitarian asset distribution and redistributive land reform (Deininger and Binswanger 1999, 2). However, in spite of these policy guidelines, there was little evidence that land reform issues affected lending by the Bank (Cassen 1994, 50).

In 1990 the World Bank published a World Development Report that concentrated on poverty issues. It summarized a great deal of research on poverty and policy and marked a renewal in the Bank's operational interest in poverty-oriented lending (Cassen 1994, 55). The document reinforced the need for redistributive land reform while acknowledging the political realities that hindered its feasibility (World Bank 1990, 64). The publication of the report was followed up by a major internal effort to embody its findings in Bank lending practice (Cassen 1994, 55).

The *World Development Report 2000/2001* on poverty and a working paper on land policy (Deininger and Binswanger 1999) marked the next step in the Bank's policy recommendations on land issues. The working paper reviewed recent research and twentieth-century experiences in reforming property rights in land. It supported land reform as a mechanism that can, in countries where the historical legacy has led to a very unequal distribution of land ownership, increase efficiency as well as equity.

The report asserted that public policy can reduce initial inequalities and increase the opportunities for poor people to benefit from growth. It continued to acknowledge that land reform could be good for poor people and for efficiency, although it concluded that only rarely did enough political support exist for coercive land reform to be implemented (World Bank 2000b, 93). An earlier draft version of the report, posted on the Internet, presented stronger support for land reform. The draft version argued that access to land is a necessary but not sufficient step to enable the poor to make productive use of the land. In addition, the institutional infrastructure must be established at the local level to ensure that land reform projects are sustainable.

Neo-liberal reforms and the associated abandonment of protection of the large (state) farm sector actually facilitated a discussion of land policy issues and opened a window to redress huge inequalities in the distribution of productive assets, according to World Bank documents (2000a, box 7.15). World Bank reports acknowledge that land rental can address obstacles faced by more efficient small farmers in rural areas of the developing world. Renting avoids the problem of finding collateral for a mortgage. Transaction costs are lower and credit, training, and technical support remain possible (Deininger and Binswanger 1999). However, the Tunisian strategy has been to rent large-scale state farms to rural large landowners for periods of twenty-five to forty years, prior to full privatization, giving them credit and technical support. Thus Tunisia missed an opportunity for market-based land reform that might have improved efficiency and equity because the state designed land and credit policies to benefit larger rather than smaller holders.

Tunisian government officials structured economic reforms to benefit their most powerful constituents. This meant ceding state-owned land to large landowners. World Bank structural adjustment loans supported this policy. Amidst the typically robot-like language of Bank documents, one can even discern

traces of Bank officials' frustration with Tunisian state agents. "The government is expressly not distributing these lands [the 0.8 million hectares of crop-
land that it owns] to improve the land assets of the rural poor" (World Bank
1995b, annex C.3, 6).

In spite of this apparent frustration, later Bank documents put a positive
spin on the adopted land policy:

> The state is also a major land-owner. . . . The [land-leasing] experience so far
> has apparently been extremely successful (more intensive cultivation, diversi-
> fied production, exports, and profits) The authorities may wish to consider
> expanding the leasing program and reassessing the costs and benefits of selling
> state lands to the private sector as another supporting measure in the estab-
> lishment of an agricultural land market. (World Bank 1996, 39)

Why did the World Bank violate its own norms when it adopted policies on
rural asset distribution and poverty in Tunisia? One World Bank official said
in an interview that state land policy was made at the presidential level and the
World Bank could not come up with a convincing argument to counter the
plans of the Tunisian officials.[4] Further discussion revealed some of the dynamics of negotiations between the World Bank and host countries. Clearly
the World Bank's focus was on maintaining the momentum of neo-liberal reform in general. It was left to the Tunisian government to deal with the distributional implications of rural structural reforms. In the case of Tunisia the
World Bank proved unwilling to base its policies on the empirical and analytical foundations of its own research.

Agricultural Economic Liberalization in
the Middle East and North Africa

In developing countries of the Middle East and North Africa (and elsewhere), state lands have been privatized to the decided advantage of large landowners:

> It was these giant state farms that were the first public enterprises to be dis-
> mantled in the early stage of post-1980 market liberalization. For this purpose
> special laws were passed. They include, for example, Syria's Law No. 10 of 1986,
> which provided for a joint venture of 25 percent share by the state and 75 per-
> cent by the private sector, as well as by Algeria's Law No. 19 of 1987, and the
> sale of most state farms in Ethiopia and Egypt in the 1990s. Those who were

4. Telephone interview by the author.

able to purchase these farms had the financial capability and political influence which are obviously unavailable to poor peasants and landless workers, resulting in the rise in concentration of landownership. (El-Ghonemy
1999, 13)

The current debates about rural Egypt focus on the equity, social, and political implications of agricultural structural adjustment (Hopkins and Westergaard 1998; Saad 1999). Current reforms are dismantling Nasser's (1952–70) socialist revolution, particularly in rural areas. The Nasserist regime was more
committed to socialism and social equity than was Tunisia under Bourguiba.
Its major effort at redistribution was the agrarian reform of 1952, which, in essence, destroyed the land base of the royal family and some two thousand large
landowners who had dominated Egypt's political and economic life (Waterbury 1993, 60).

Nasser's ambitious agrarian reform program of the 1950s was intended to
free poor peasants from a life of virtual servitude to wealthy owners. The reforms granted some one million families quasi-property rights—secure tenancy
at fixed rents on properties taken over from the country's largest landowners.
It also provided an organizational structure through which the interests of
peasants could be articulated and defended in both administrative and political settings (Springborg 1990).

Rent ceilings and secure tenancy did initially benefit an impoverished peasantry, but over time they contributed to the stagnation of agricultural productivity. By 1985 land values had reached at least 20,000 Egyptian pounds per
feddan (1.038 acres), while rents remained fixed at less than 80 pounds per feddan (Hinnebusch 1993, 21). Frequently tenants did not have sufficient resources
to increase production. The need for agrarian reform was evident and mounting; however, political elites could choose among several types of agrarian
economic reform. Throughout the 1980s fear of political instability prevented
the government from confronting the struggle between landlords and tenants, many of whom had cultivated rent-controlled land for generations. These
struggles centered on the amount of compensation to be granted tenants under
new rent laws.

In 1992, the regime changed the law governing owner-tenant relations and,
especially after 1997, began evicting tenants from their plots. In the end, under
the auspices of a structural adjustment program, the interests of the owners
triumphed while those of the tenants were practically ignored. The compensation paid to tenants amounted to only one-fifth of the sum considered during
debates on the subject (Hinnebusch 1993, 22). In the words of Sayed al-Toukhi

(quoted in "Freethought Traditions" 1995), an official from an Egyptian human rights organization, "The government is slowly pushing three million farmers off their land and selling the land to 100,000 wealthy landowners." Abolishing the tenancy law was the first step in replacing small peasant production with larger-scale capitalist enterprise (Hinnebusch 1993). The Egyptian agrarian reform of 1952 (Ireton 1998, 63) had spurred improvement in access to land; the 1990s saw the end of that trend.

The general dynamics of agrarian economic liberalization in Egypt have been similar to those in Tunisia:

> The program of reform . . . fails to recognize the complex way in which rural politics and the gender division of labor affect agricultural modernization. . . . Landowners can shape production systems for export crops and reap the benefits of comparative advantage. [In this approach] Rural poor and landless, those dispossessed by and marginalized by market deregulation, can either work in the countryside or migrate to towns in search of employment. This rationale is premised on economic growth and a local bourgeoisie which is prepared to invest rather than strip the countryside of its assets. Yet the linking of agricultural development and income generation to the vagaries of the external market has failed to deliver projected rates of growth. (Bush 1998, 89)

The prospects for poverty reduction are limited at best in the new market arrangements:

> The sad result [of Egyptian agrarian economic liberalization] is increasing poverty and inequality of income distribution in rural Egypt. . . . [I estimate] that the adopted economic policy reforms have brought poverty incidence back to its 1950 level of 56 percent, prior to the distributive land reform policy which was introduced in 1952. (El-Ghonemy 1999, 15)

Market economic reforms have also been associated with growing landlord power in Egypt's national institutions. During the reform period, peasants have lost representation in parliament, in the political and administrative structures that make and implement agricultural policy, and in local politics, as well as in government jobs, while the state has advanced the interests of large landowners (Springborg 1991; Fandy 1994; Saad 1999). In addition, the disaffected Islamist opposition is quite visible in rural areas, even more than it is in Tunisia. The type of landlord system and the increasing landlessness associated with the Egyptian agricultural market reforms provide an impetus to this opposition (Bush 1998, 92).

In Morocco, also, agrarian polices have benefited large landlords and other economic elites, including the king and his entourage. "The King and his political allies—high military officers, the urban political and economic elites, and rural notables—have been the major beneficiaries of Morocco's agrarian policies since independence."[5] Structural adjustment programs, followed strictly in Morocco since 1982, have perpetuated the bias toward the rural elite. "The concentration of investments in modern, export-oriented farming and the neglect of traditional agriculture, from which 90 percent of Moroccan peasants still derive their income, led to a massive exodus from rural areas, [and] a dramatic expansion of urban shantytowns." Peasants lack political representation, and violence and repression are used when the poor and landless mobilize to obtain land (Maghraoui 2001, 77).

The Moroccan case adds another dimension to the discussion of agrarian economic liberalization, equity, and rural politics: the issue of irrigation. The regime has moved to privatize state, collective, and religious orders' lands. It has also introduced broader agricultural sector policies, including a national irrigation program supported by the World Bank. In this arid region of the world, climatic conditions are tremendously important and have a major impact on agricultural production regardless of state policies. The program created agricultural water-users' associations, and aimed to irrigate one million hectares by the year 2000. Under the leadership of the Ministry of Agriculture, the program seeks to improve rural conditions through demand-driven, coordinated investments in small- and medium-scale irrigation and complementary community infrastructure, including rural roads, water supply and sanitation, electrification, and health and education facilities (World Bank 2001b).

In this monarchial regime, as in the past, the government took the initiative, defined "the rules of the game," and maintained oversight of these irrigation projects and water-users' associations. The potential impact of these irrigation programs is quite significant, and to date they appear to perpetuate the elite bias that one finds in other aspects of agrarian economic liberalization policies that pay insufficient attention to rural power relations (Bennis and Sadeq 1998).

Overall, power relations probably affect rural markets most strongly in the realm of land distribution. Due to power disparities, new markets in land rarely culminate in access to land for the most economically efficient. Land distribution is measured in terms of the Gini coefficient, which ranges from zero to one; the larger the index, the greater the degree of inequality in the size distribution of landholdings. Table 10 gives these figures for Tunisia and Egypt, before and after market reforms were instituted.

---

5. Will Swearingen, *Moroccan Mirages: Agrarian Dreams and Deceptions, 1912–1986* (Princeton, N.J.: Princeton University Press, 1987), quoted in Maghraoui 2001, 77.

Table 10. Changes in the Distribution of Landholding

Country	Year	Gini Coefficient
Tunisia		
Before Market Reform	1980	.60
After Market Reform	1986–1990	.64
Egypt		
Before Market Reform	1982	.57
After Market Reform	1990	.60

The earlier Tunisian figure is from El-Ghonemy 1996, 4; the later is from Deininger and Olinto 1999, 24. Egyptian figures are from Ireton 1998, 61.

Countries in the Middle East and North Africa generally resist reporting measures of land inequality. Such data are virtually always absent from the Food and Agricultural Organization's (FAO) studies produced at the beginning of each decade. The data have become even more difficult to attain since the major land privatizations of the 1990s.[6]

The increase in the Gini coefficient in Egypt between 1982 and 1990 reflects the privatization of state lands during that period (Ireton 1998, 61). Analysts fear that the new land tenure laws implemented in 1997 have significantly increased land concentration (Hopkins and Westergaard 1998).

Customary Tenure Systems, Food Production, and Gender in Africa

Customary land tenure systems are dominant in most countries of Africa. Land tenure is based on the diverse traditions developed by ethnic groups to fit the particular (usually semi-arid) area's socio-ecological context (El-Ghonemy 1999, 7). In these traditions, land is owned by the community rather than the individual. The ability of outsiders to sell or rent land is restricted. Traditional village authorities may influence how land is allocated among households (El-Ghonemy 1999, 17; Deininger 2000, 4–5). Structural adjustment programs intended to use markets to increase efficiency in resource use aim to privatize these commons and establish Western-style individual freehold titles. Land has been privatized even though customary tenure systems are flexible enough to adapt to modern agrarian markets based on export crops while maintaining

6. When I asked about the subject, the Tunisian government revoked my research clearance. It apparently also resists attempts by multilateral agencies to place land equity on the development agenda.

their central role in food production (El-Ghonemy 1999). According to recent World Bank studies, the inefficiency of customary tenure systems has been exaggerated

> for a number of reasons. First, arable land (in contrast to pasture and forest or fishing grounds) is, in the large majority of communal tenure systems, cultivated by individuals who may even enjoy inheritable rights. This implies that the static (and maybe even dynamic) efficiency losses possibly associated with communal tenure may be quite limited. Second, communal resource ownership is often maintained because it either provides public goods or allows [individuals] to take advantage of synergies that would be difficult to provide under fully individualized cultivation. . . . Finally, while communal systems prohibit land transactions to outsiders, rental and often even sale within the community (and possibly beyond) is normally allowed, providing scope for efficiency-enhancing transfers (Deininger 2000, 6).

The World Bank considers Uganda to be a successful case of agricultural structural adjustment (Deininger and Okidi 2001). The development of markets in and titles to land did not lead to the concentration of landholdings in few hands. The land rental markets helped to equalize land access. Removing implicit taxation on exports and liberalizing the market made recovery in export crops possible, and a boom in international coffee prices in the mid-1990s provided a boost for producers. Although there was regional variation, with the north generally stagnant and engaged in traditional farming, agricultural production for the market, in which different income groups participated, played an important role in economic growth in Uganda in the 1990s (Deininger and Okidi 2001, 125).

This success, however, is marred by the extent to which commercialization in Uganda benefits men at women's expense, since men are more likely than women to control the income from cash crops (Mackinnon and Reinikka 2000, 11). Therefore, women may benefit relatively more from increases in domestic productivity than from increases in cash crops.

In addition, political power and corruption played an important role during the privatization of customary land tenure in Uganda. "Money does enter into the issuance of titling where district land committees (DLCs) are corrupt or where the condition of issuance of the lease includes demonstration of financial capacity to develop the land" (Kigula 1993). Large landowners, whose properties often reflect past political power rather than market forces, are also not always interested in farming (Mackinnon and Reinikka 2000, 36). In two districts of the country nearly half the buyers of over 100,000 hectares of land were members of parliament, government officials and senior police officers, and urbanites related to influential policymakers. These new owners prevented the traditional users of the land from grazing their animals and producing food crops (El-Ghonemy 1999, 18).

The Ivory Coast's experience of agricultural structural adjustment was more negative than that of Uganda. Implementation of the policies has been constricted by the country's confinement within the CFA franc zone. Poverty and inequality have increased, because price liberalization was badly timed and the production of food crops dropped sharply when land tenure was privatized. Violent disputes over land between Ivorian rural dwellers and immigrants from neighboring countries have also complicated agricultural policy.

In August 1999, when world prices for coffee and cocoa had dropped 40 percent below the previous season's, the Ivorian government abruptly canceled the price-fixing mechanism for these crops, which had been in place for thirty-seven years (EIU 2000, 14), causing sharp losses for export crop farmers. Structural adjustment also reduced food production. The yams, cassava, millet, and sorghum that provide rural people with most of their calories have traditionally been produced on communally held lands. With privatization, these areas have been converted to the production of export crops. The net result has been a sharp fall in both food productivity and caloric intake (El-Ghonemy 1999, 18). Mounting rural tensions, including conflicts with immigrants from Burkina Faso, were part of the backdrop of the December 1999 coup d'état (EIU 2000, 14).

Summarizing some of the pitfalls of agrarian economic liberalization in Uganda, Malawi, and the Ivory Coast, El-Ghonemy emphasizes the varied impact of structural adjustment policies on different income and gender groups:

> The experience of several privatizing countries suggests (i) the vulnerability of individual owners to the loss of land to urban speculators as well as to mortgage and heavy indebtedness; (ii) the weakening of women's customary rights in land and command over food; (iii) the shift away from food crops toward cash/export crops. Moreover, because of transaction costs, the land buyers are businessmen, politicians, senior civil servants, members of the armed forces and larger landowners. (El-Ghonemy 1999, 18)

Market-Assisted Land Reform

In an effort to address land equity and efficiency issues in some developing countries (Brazil, Columbia, Kenya, South Africa, and the Philippines), the World Bank has recently begun supporting "market-friendly" land reform programs. "In a market assisted land reform, beneficiaries receive a combination of grants and loans from the public and private sectors which they use to negotiate the purchase of land from willing sellers. The willing seller–willing buyer framework of market assisted land reform contrasts with government directed land reform in which the government disposes the land from a large farm and gives it free of charge to the poor" (World Bank 2001a, 1).

The World Bank hopes that market-assisted land reform will provide governments with a way to deal with highly unequal distribution of land in a way that does not undermine the security of property rights and the functioning of factor markets (Deininger 2000, 73). These programs are too new for full evaluation and are being adjusted based on on-going experiences in countries implementing them. Scholars associated with the World Bank are obviously optimistic about land reform based on market forces. They hope that this approach will close the gap between the rhetoric and the practice of asset distribution so apparent in standard structural adjustment programs. This optimism is refuted by some scholars (Kay 1999). Familiar issues of rural power and politics not addressed in the approach have already started to crop up. In Brazil, landlords sell low-quality land (El-Ghonemy 1999, 14). Large landowners in the country, who lobbied for the policy, seem the most pleased with the project, rather than the landless and land-poor:

> Land owners are quite pleased with the project. It pays for their land in cash rather than in twenty-year bonds. It allows them to negotiate the price of the land, and to determine which plots to sell. Cédula de Terra allows landowners to dump less-desirable plots in return for immediate cash, protecting their prime holdings—idle or not—from disappropriation. (Plevin 1999, 2)

In other countries, frequently the local power monopoly of landlords, high transaction costs for the landless, and the activities of the politically well-connected frustrate market-assisted land transfers to poor peasants (El-Ghonemy 1999).

Conclusion

Overall, poverty reduction strategies that have actually been implemented with the support of the World Bank have not emphasized a reduction in unequal access to land (Deininger 2000, 126), despite a long history of official land policy positions to the contrary and recent analyses emphasizing that initial asset inequality has significant negative effects on long-term growth (Deininger and Olinto 1999). Structural adjustment programs that ignore asset

distribution permit, and may actually promote through Bank funding, the upward redistribution of land. The results of these policies refute theoretical assertions that structural adjustment benefits all rural income groups.

The neo-liberal approach also assumes that agricultural adjustment programs will encourage smallholders to produce profitable export crops, but such
programs do not do enough to facilitate their broad integration into new market arrangements. In addition, food production may drop and women in particular may be left behind during these agrarian reforms.

An alternative to neo-liberalism in the countryside needs to be formulated
and implemented. Market-friendly land reform does not appear to be it because it fails to address landlord power, which undermines the standard approach. Agrarian reform must involve state regulation to overcome the failure
of markets to deliver equitable, just, and productive outcomes in rural development. A shared-growth approach that ensures access to land for small and
medium peasants and benefits them in its broader agricultural policies would
be a start.

The neo-liberal transformation that we are witnessing needlessly concentrates rural assets and hinders the ability of the majority of rural dwellers to
deal with their problems, cooperate with each other, and cope with political
authorities and economic elites during a period of major asset redistribution
(Mitchell 1999). The loss of social capital (Putnam 1995) among the small peasantry in the countryside sheds light on one aspect of the linkage between market economic reform and political change.

❖ 6 ❖
_____

THE POLITICS OF EMPOWERING
THE WINNERS OF ECONOMIC REFORM

As a consequence of neo-liberal reforms, the economies of many developing countries are currently undergoing major structural transformations that could profoundly and permanently alter the distribution of assets. Some of these policies (e.g., privatization in both rural and urban areas) often lead to a major worsening of asset inequality. The new market arrangements have important implications for political organization, yet much of current theorizing in the political development literature eschews economic variables while assuming that market reforms will enhance democratic prospects.

Certainly there are many cases in which market reforms and democratization seem to have proceeded together: India—market reforms since 1984 with maintenance of democracy; Mexico—reforms since 1982 with slow loosening of single-party dominance; Turkey—reforms since 1983 and the institutionalization of a democratic process; Spain—democratization and market reforms; Portugal—democratization followed by market reforms; Argentina—reforms since 1983 with alternance of political parties in elections; Chile—market reform and democracy after Pinochet; Poland—the same after the Communist regime; Korea—market reforms followed by democratization. Yet in many of these countries, which are considered part of the third wave of democracy, democratic rule remains uncertain. Karl (1990) has emphasized that making pacts with the elite is especially conducive to democratization, with guarantees in particular for traditional ruling classes. Others emphasize that capital must be restructured with market reforms in order to establish its dominance economically and politically (O'Brien and Cammack 1985). The emerging democracies lose their promise as a route to social justice. Labor has been marginalized under the new democratic regimes (Collier 1999a, 197).

In rural areas of many developing countries, economic liberalization seems to undermine democratic prospects. Frances Hagopian analyzed the persis-

tence of traditional politics in Brazil's new democracy. She argued that rural elites exploited a protracted process of democratization to transmit and
enhance decades-old patterns of political influence. Ensconced within positions of power within the ruling party and the opposition, traditional elites
"thwarted progressive reforms, bolstered pervasive clientelism, fought success-
fully to retain political institutions that favor conservative actors, and perpetuated non-democratic practices in the new democracy. A clientelistic partial regime subverted democracy in the countryside (quoted in Encarnacion
2000, 494).

Kurtz (1996) argued that national democracy in Chile has been purchased
at the cost of the political underdevelopment of the peasantry. Neo-liberalism
disrupted rural social structure and gravely hindered associational life in the
countryside. Political acquiescence in the rural sector helped sustain pluralism
and elections nationally.

In addition, the electoral regimes in some of these transitions seem to suggest the reconfiguration of authoritarianism as much as new democratic developments. Movements toward electoral democracy have often been combined
with rampant violations of individual liberties. Larry Diamond writes that "to
varying but alarming degrees human rights are flagrantly abused, ethnic and
other minorities suffer not only discrimination but murderous violence; power
is heavily if not regally concentrated in the executive branch; and parties, leg-
islators, executives and judicial systems are thoroughly corrupt" (quoted in Encarnacion 2000, 13).

Fareed Zakaria (1997) used the term "illiberal democracy" to describe a
growing number of countries that combine free and fair elections with a fusion
of powers, a weak rule of law, and a lack of protection of basic liberties of
speech, assembly, religion, and property. The spectrum of illiberal democracies
ranged from modest offenders like Argentina to near-tyrannies like Kazakstan
and Belarus, with countries like Romania and Bangladesh in between. In a
similar vein, Clifford Geertz described the emerging political economy of the
Arab world as the marriage of Smithian economics and Hobbesian politics
(quoted in Vandewalle 1986, 13).

The term "delegative democracy" also partially captures the political patterns associated with market reforms. Guillermo O'Donnell coined the term
to depict a "new animal, a subtype of existing democracies, which has yet to
be theorized" (O'Donnell 1994, 55). In a delegative democracy an elected president concentrates power in the executive branch, subordinates the legislature,
and rules by decree. O'Donnell also points out that implementing democracy

under conditions of increasing inequality leads to a policy process further biased in favor of highly organized and economically powerful interests. In the end, authoritarian practices reassert themselves.

The lexicon of terms to describe the numerous emerging regimes that are obviously not transitional democracies is shifting toward the authoritarian end of the spectrum. Martha Olcott and Marina Ottaway use the term "semi-authoritarianism" to describe regimes that combine formal democracy (with constitutions that provide for the separation of powers and contested presidential and parliamentary elections) and a modicum of political openness with fundamental authoritarian tendencies. The defining characteristic of these regimes is "the existence and persistence of mechanisms that effectively prevent the transfer of power through elections from the hands of the incumbent leaders or party to a new political elite or political organization" (Olcott and Ottaway 1999, 1). The geographical scope of this semi-authoritarian trend is as wide as that noted in Huntington's *The Third Wave* (1991):

> Such regimes abound in the former Soviet Union: in countries like Kazakhstan or Azerbaijan, for example, former communist bosses have transformed themselves into elected presidents, but in reality they remain strongmen whose power is barely checked by weak democratic institutions. Semi-authoritarian regimes are also numerous in sub-Saharan Africa, where most of the multiparty elections of the 1990s have failed to produce working parliaments, or other institutions capable of holding the executive accountable. In the Middle East, tentative political openings in Algeria, Morocco, and Yemen appear to be leading to the consolidation of semi-authoritarian regimes rather than to democracy, following a pattern first established by Egypt. In the Balkans, the communist regimes have disappeared, but democracy remains a distant hope even in countries that are at peace. Even more worrisome is the example of Latin America, where steady progress toward democracy has been interrupted by the new semi-authoritarianism of Peru and Venezuela. (Olcott and Ottaway 1999, 1)

Clearly the number of regimes that are emerging from ISI populism with fundamental authoritarian traits poses an analytic challenge that the current literature is only beginning to address. The democracy literature's focus on the autonomy of the political dimension and the actions of political elites does not provide a path to answer the basic question: Why do some regimes that are attempting to develop a market-oriented economy become democratic while many others resist democratization or become authoritarian? To answer this question we must look to political economy, understand the shift in preferences of individual and collective actors, and better appreciate institutional constraints:

> Not democratic transition games but political economy becomes crucially important: the shift of preferences, resources, constraints, and opportunities that resulted from ongoing economic crisis, from the reordering of the world economy, and from the crisis of socialist and statist alternatives. (Collier 1999a, 197)

In addition, the actual rather than inferred relationship between economics and politics is likely best understood through in-depth case studies and local-level analysis instead of the cross-national aggregate data studies that have been the foundation of theory building at the grand level. This study of Tunisia has sought to advance theory and understanding of the relationship between market reforms and political change by emphasizing the importance of fieldwork and of carefully tracing the impact of state economic policy and ideology on political organization within a single country.

Tunisia

Perhaps of all the states in the Middle East and North Africa, Tunisia appeared to be the most likely to develop a liberal democracy. Its own leaders have historically pointed to a modern constitution that was first promulgated over a hundred years ago. Thus, Tunisia's elites have claimed that the country has long had a legal tradition and spirit among its people that is conducive to democratic rule (Anderson 1991, 255). The country's main Islamist movement has been comparatively moderate and formally committed to democracy. A generation of scholars, working primarily in the modernization school, provided a base for an understanding of Tunisia's single-party system that emphasized a liberal, pluralist direction of political change. Regime elites in particular would inculcate mass behavioral and attitudinal changes that supported democracy. In his 1965 *Tunisia since Independence,* a central text on Tunisia's single party, Clement Henry Moore introduced his discussion with the observation that "Tunisia's ruling Neo-Destour Party has achieved the most effective regime in the Afro-Asian world for leading its people toward a modern society" (quoted in Anderson 1990, 57).

The first few years of Ben Ali's presidency, 1987–90, appeared to vindicate early predictions of regime change. Pluralist, competitive democracy was the major plank of the new president, and the national pact whose signing he organized in 1988 endorsed it. He presided over the renovation of his party, now renamed the Rassemblement Constitutionnel Démocratique (RCD), replacing numerous cadres, and also recognized several new parties. In some accounts, the legislative and presidential elections of 1989 signaled a democratic transition that fit into the "third wave" of democratization occurring worldwide. The prevailing democratization literature focused on the exact choices and agreements that Tunisia's elite seemed to be making, and the way in which they inculcated democratic values.

Moreover, Tunisia's economic choices and socioeconomic trends, according to prevailing theory, suggested that democratization might even be rapid. After the abrupt collapse of ISI populism in 1969, Tunisia underwent two phases of economic reform. The gradual period of market reforms, from 1970 to 1986, improved aggregate economic growth, but largely avoided fundamental structural changes. However, Ben Ali's ascension to power led to the intensification of market-oriented policies. "One of Ben Ali's first moves was to make sweeping reforms in the top management of the parastatals, replacing established party members with younger technocrats whose training, ideology, and personal interests were compatible with greater economic integration with transnational capitalism. . . . The new ruling elite was united not so much by its institutional basis as by a common allegiance to the [economic] reform policies" (Payne 1991, 144–45). Tunisia has been consistently lauded by the World Bank for its commitment to neo-liberal reforms. Aggregate economic growth rates have been high, and Tunisia is considered a star pupil of the international financial institutions.

U.S. government agencies, international financial institutions, and much of the literature on political development harbored the hope that markets would foster democracy in places like Tunisia. However, in the 1990s, Tunisian authorities grew more intolerant of opposition of any kind. Rather than democratization or liberalization, the period of accelerated marketization in Tunisia has been associated with the hardening of authoritarianism. Indeed in early 2002, President Ben Ali amended the constitution to permit a fourth five-year presidential term, thereby effectively undoing his abolition of life presidency, a reform he had trumpeted upon taking power in 1987.

The familiar explanation for this lack of democratic progress in Tunisia centers on Islamic culture and the country's proximity to Algeria's war pitting Islamists against the state. However, there are other plausible explanations that shed light on the links between economic and political change in the developing world. Little attention has been paid to the worsening of income distribution that often accompanies neo-liberal reforms, and that hinders the prospects of democratization. Nor has there been much focus on the clientelist, authoritarian, and corporatist policies and strategies that are common features of neo-liberal transformation.

Neo-liberal reforms in Tunisia provided the material basis on which authoritarianism was reconfigured in a less populist form. While partially addressing a real need for economic reform, Ben Ali's economic policies redistributed both income and access to agricultural land upward, diminished the influence of trade unions, and increased the power of private capital, partially through rampant rent-seeking. Neo-liberal reform was not the only approach available to Tunisian leaders. Their choice of policies reflected the party's returning to its roots as a party of rural notables. The urban offshoots of these rural elites benefited most from the period of gradual economic liberalization, as they diversified their investments beyond agriculture to transport, construction, and hotel management, aided by preferential access to government and private credit (Anderson 1986, 240). More recent state economic projects further solidified the interests of large landowners and the most powerful elements of the urban bourgeoisie. The state party realigned and solidified the social underpinning of the state through policies that benefited these dominant economic groups.

Neo-liberal economic reforms also facilitated the rehabilitation of state corporatism in Tunisia. In recent literature the emergence of a neo-corporatist partial regime is deemed beneficial to market reforms and democracy. O'Donnell and Schmitter (1986) advocate that consultation, cooperation, and consensus on macroeconomic policy be institutionalized, involving peak representation from organized capital, trade unions, and the state. "Concerted" neo-corporatist policies supposedly can manage and resolve the socioeconomic conflicts associated with transitions from dictatorship to political democracy (O'Donnell and Schmitter 1986, 45–47).

However, the present study comes to nearly opposite conclusions. Neo-corporatist policies have helped state elites reconfigure authoritarianism during market transitions. The trend may be toward state corporatism, not societal corporatism. In the 1970s and early 1980s, the Tunisian national labor union (UGTT) challenged Bourguiba's corporatist arrangements and authoritarian polity. The 1978 general strike and calls for democratic reforms set the process of democratization in Tunisia in motion. However, by the late 1980s, the UGTT had begun participating in new corporatist institutions. Its leadership agreed to concerted neo-corporatist arrangements with organized capital and the state, despite a drop in labor's share of national income and increasing unemployment. The UGTT also renewed support for the RCD. Economic crisis and labor's loss of bargaining power during Tunisia's neo-liberal transformation had led it to prefer authoritarian rule to democracy. Significantly, the labor movement never formed a political party that might have become a real threat to RCD hegemony.

The electoral regime in Tunisia has also been reconfigured to accompany the new economic strategy. Initially, Ben Ali's political opening fueled Tunisia's incipient pluralism. However, the ethos of the regime has turned out to be much more in the corporatist-authoritarian than the liberal democratic political tradition. According to Schmitter (1974, 96–97), corporatists believe that they will be able to adjust the clash of societal interests and render them all subservient to the public good (defined by the superior wisdom of the autocratic leader and technocratic planners). They seek to limit (or eliminate), co-opt, control, and coordinate the factions. From the results of the 1989, 1994, and 1999 elections, Ben Ali's electoral system appears to be designed to permit an orbital cloud of opposition parties that cannot significantly affect the hegemonic role of the RCD. It is intended to form a consensual authoritarianism with legal opposition parties referring to themselves as parties of support of the regime in the "new era."

The economic and political projects that have characterized recent changes in Tunisia have been facilitated by state efforts to curtail the country's pressure regime. Coercion and repression played a role in getting the UGTT to accept Ben Ali's emerging corporate-authoritarian order. Even more state violence has been necessary to contain the Islamist resistance. Since being unleashed against al-Nahda in the early 1990s, the security apparatus has been used to intimidate wide swaths of Tunisian society. Freedom of the press, of association, and of speech have been dramatically foreclosed in the past decade. Civil society has been subjugated to the "national consensus."

Finally, and most importantly, this book has attempted to contribute to the literature on the links between market economic reforms and political change by focusing on the local level. The Tebourba community study revealed the retraditionalization of local politics and the revival of clientelism during state-led economic liberalization. The state's promotion of cultural traditionalism in rural communities helps sustain the new authoritarianism that has emerged on the national level. The regime revived cultural traditionalism in order to contain the tensions caused by its economic policies. Reeling from relative material losses and drawn back into patron-client relations and Islamic welfare mechanisms, the small peasantry withdrew from formal political institutions that had become obvious vehicles for large landowners.

One of the major misfortunes of the Tunisian case is that a different approach to market-oriented policies, one less tilted in favor of rural and urban economic elites, might have given subordinate groups a better chance to use increasing marketization to press for a more liberal, plural, and democratic society. Instead neo-liberal reforms reinforced corporatism, clientelism, and authoritarianism.

The stability of the new, less populist authoritarianism in Tunisia is still in question. Continued economic growth, well-managed repression, and fear of a situation like that in Algeria may keep the Tunisian Islamists at bay. However, the RCD is increasingly recognized as having abandoned its historical commitments to equity and become a party representing the interests of rural notables, the urban bourgeoisie, and transnational finance. Labor (the base of the national labor union, if not the leadership) and the small peasantry are muttering complaints about their lack of strong representation in the hegemonic party political system. Moreover, European Union accords will force more privatizations and higher unemployment over the next ten years, which could provoke workers to greater resistance. The closed political space and lack of civil liberties are stifling to everyone. On the other hand, Ben Ali's regime has proven that it can handle many of these challenges, and may be able to for a long period of time, absent major events provoking a break.

BIBLIOGRAPHY

Alesina, Alberto. 1996. "The Political Economy of Macroeconomic Stabilizations and Income Inequality: Myths and Reality." Working paper, International Monetary Fund, Washington D.C.

Alexander, Chris. 1996. "State, Labor, and the New Global Economy in Tunisia." In *North Africa: Development and Reform in a Changing Global Economy,* ed. Dirk J. Vandewalle. New York: St. Martin's Press.

Almond, Gabriel, and James Coleman. 1960. *Politics in Developing Areas.* Princeton, N.J.: Princeton University Press.

Amin, Samir. 1970. *The Maghreb in the Modern World: Algeria, Tunisia, Morocco.* Translated by Michael Perl. Harmondsworth: Penguin.

———. 1998. *Capitalism in the Age of Globalization.* London: Zed.

Anderson, Lisa. 1986. *The State and Social Transformation in Tunisia and Libya, 1830–1980.* Princeton, N.J.: Princeton University Press.

———. 1990. "Policy-Making and Theory Building: American Political Science and the Islamic Middle East." In *Theory, Politics, and the Arab World: Critical Responses,* ed. Hisham Sharabi. New York: Routledge.

———. 1991. "Political Pacts, Liberalism, and Democracy: The Tunisian National Pact of 1988." *Government and Opposition* 26, no. 2 (spring): 244–60.

Ashford, Douglas. 1967. *National Development and Local Reform: Political Participation in Morocco, Tunisia, and Pakistan.* Princeton, N.J.: Princeton University Press.

Association Française pour l'Avancement des Sciences. 1896. *La Tunisie.* 2 vols. Paris: Berger-Levrault.

Attia, Habib. 1966. "L'Évolution des Structures Agraires en Tunisie depuis 1962." *Revue Tunisienne des Sciences Sociales,* no. 7: 33–58.

Axelrod, Robert. 1986. "An Evolutionary Approach to Norms." *American Political Science Review* 80, no. 4 (December): 1095–1111.

Baird, Mark, and Deborah Wetzel. 1995. "Reducing Poverty: Lessons from Experience." World Bank Staff Report.

Bardham, Pranab, Samuel Bowles, and Herbert Gintis. 1998. *Wealth Inequality, Wealth Constraints, and Economic Performance.* Amherst: University of Massachusetts Press.

Bardin, Pierre. 1965. *La Vie d'un Douar: Essai sur la Vie dans les Grandes Plaines de la Haute Medjerda, Tunisie.* Paris: La Haye.

Barro, Robert J. 1996. "Democracy and Growth." *Journal of Economic Growth* 1 (March): 1–27.

Beer, Linda. 1999. "Income Inequality and Transnational Corporate Penetration." *Journal of World-Systems Research* 5, no. 1 (spring): 1–25.

Bellin, Eva. 1995. "Civil Society in Formation." In *Civil Society in the Middle East,* ed. Augustus R. Norton, vol. 1. Leiden: E. J. Brill.

Bennis, Abdelhadi, and Houria Tazi Sadeq. 1998. "Local Participation in Water Management: Empowering Communities to Take the Lead. Morocco." In *Water and Population Dynamics: Case Studies and Policy Implications,* ed. Alex de Sherbinin and Victoria Dompka with Lars Bromley. Washington, D.C.: World Conservation Union, American Association for the Advancement of Science.

Berry, Albert, and William Cline. 1979. *Agrarian Structure and Productivity in Developing Countries.* Baltimore: Johns Hopkins University Press.

Birdsall, Nancy, Carol Graham, and Richard Sabot, eds. 1998. *Beyond Tradeoffs: Market Reforms and Equitable Growth in Latin America.* Washington, D.C.: Inter-American Development Bank, The Brookings Institution.

Boris, G. 1951. *Documents Linguistiques et Ethnographiques sur une Région du Sud Tunisien.* Paris: Nafouz.

Boswell, Terry, and William J. Dixon. 1993. "Marx's Theory of Rebellion: A Cross-national Analysis of Class Exploitation, Economic Development, and Violent Revolt." *American Sociological Review* 58, no. 5 (October): 681–702.

Boukhra, Ridha. 1976. "La Problématique de la Communauté Rurale au Maghreb: Quelques Observations sur le Changement Social dans la Communauté Villageoise de Hammamet." *Revue Tunisienne des Sciences Sociales* 45: 11–48.

Bourgignon, François, and Christian Morrisson. 1992. *Adjustment and Equity in Developing Countries: A New Approach.* Paris: Development Centre of the Organisation for Economic Co-operation and Development.

Braun, Denny. 1991. *The Rich Get Richer: The Rise of Income Inequality in the United States and the World.* Chicago: Nelson-Hall.

Brown, Leon Carl. 1964. "Stages in the Process of Change." In *Tunisia: The Politics of Modernization,* ed. C. A. Micaud. New York: Praeger.

Bruno, Michael, Martin Ravallion, and Lyn Squire. 1995. *Equity and Growth in Developing Countries: Old and New Perspectives on the Policy Issues.* Washington, D.C.: International Monetary Fund.

Bush, Ray. 1998. "Hegemony in the Periphery: Community and Exclusion in an Upper Egyptian Village." In *Directions of Change in Rural Egypt,* ed. Nicholas S. Hopkins and Kirsten Westergaard. Cairo: The American University in Cairo Press.

Cammack, Paul. 1997. *Capitalism and Democracy in the Third World.* Leicester: Leicester University Press.

Cammack, Paul, and Philip O'Brien. 1985. *Generals in Retreat.* Manchester: Manchester University Press.

Cassen, Robert. 1994. *Does Aid Work?* Oxford: Clarendon.

Chalmers, Douglas A., et al., eds. 1997. *The New Politics of Inequality in Latin America: Rethinking Participation and Representation.* Oxford: Oxford University Press.

Chater, Khalifa. 1978. *La Mahella de Zarrouk au Sahel.* Tunis: Université de Tunis.

Chaudhry, Kirin. 1992. "Economic Liberalization in Oil-Exporting Countries: Iraq and

Saudi Arabia." In *Privatization and Liberalization in the Middle East,* ed. Iliya Harik and Denis Sullivan. Bloomington: Indiana University Press.

———. 1994. "The Middle East and the Political Economy of Development." *Items* 48, nos. 2–3 (June–September): 41–49.

Collier, Ruth Berins. 1999a. *Paths towards Democracy.* Cambridge: Cambridge University Press.

———. 1999b. "The Transformation of Labor-Based One Partyism at the End of the Twentieth Century: The Case of Mexico." In *The Awkward Embrace: One-Party Domination and Democracy,* ed. Hermann Giliomee and Charles Simkins. Australia: Harwood Academic Publishers.

Commander, Simon, ed. 1989. *Structural Adjustment and Agriculture.* London: Overseas Development Institute.

Cornia, Giovanni Andrea, Richard Jolly, and Frances Stewart, eds. 1987. *Adjustment with a Human Face.* Oxford: Clarendon.

Cuisenier, Jean. 1961. *L'Ansarine: Contribution à la Sociologie du Développement.* Paris: Presses Universitaires de France.

Dahl, Reynold P. 1971. "Agricultural Development Strategies in a Small Economy: The Case of Tunisia." Staff paper, USAID. A version of this paper was published in *Options Méditerranéenes* 11 (February 1972): 105–12, and is available at <http://ressources.ciheam.org/om/pdf/r11/CI010669.pdf>, accessed June 24, 2002.

Dahl, Robert. 1989. *Democracy and Its Critics.* New Haven, Conn.: Yale University Press.

Daoud, Arezki. 1999. "Opposition Parties in Tunisia at the Eve of the Elections." *North Africa Journal,* no. 66 (September 30). At <http://www.north-africa.com/archives/docs/093099A.htm>, accessed August 6, 2002.

Dardel, Jean-Baptiste, and Chedli Klibi Slaheddine. 1955. "Une Faubourg Clandestin de Tunis: Le Djebel Lahmar." *Les Cahiers de Tunisie* 10: 211–24.

Deininger, Klaus. 2000. "Land Policy and Administration: Lessons Learned and New Challenges for the Bank's Agenda." Preliminary version of a paper for the World Bank Land Policy and Administration Thematic Group.

Deininger, Klaus, and Hans Binswanger. 1999. "The Evolution of the World Bank's Land Policy: Principles, Experiences, and Future Challenges." *World Bank Research Observer* 14, no. 2: 247–76. Also at <http://www.worldbank.org/research/journals/wbro/obsaug99/article5.pdf>, accessed August 6, 2002.

Deininger, Klaus, and John Okidi. 2000. "Land Policy and Administration: Lessons Learned and New Challenges for the Bank's Development Agenda." World Bank Land Policy Thematic Group.

———. 2001. "Growth and Poverty Reduction in Uganda, 1992–2000: Panel Data Evidence." World Bank paper. A version is at <http://www.econ.ox.ac.uk/CSAEadmin/conferences/2002-UPaGiSSA/papers/okidi-csae2002.pdf>, accessed June 24, 2002.

Deininger, Klaus, and Pedro Olinto. 1999. "Asset Distribution and Growth: New Panel Estimates." World Bank mimeograph.

Deininger, Klaus, and Lyn Squire. 1996. "A New Data Set Measuring Inequality." *World Bank Economic Review* 10, no. 3 (September): 565–91.

De Montety, Henri. 1973. "Old Families and New Elites in Tunisia." In *Man, State, and Society in the Contemporary Maghrib,* ed. I. William Zartman. New York: Praeger.

Denny, Frederick. 1987. *Islam.* San Francisco: Harper and Row.

Denoeux, Guilain. 1994. "Tunisie: Les Élections Présidentielles et Législatives, 20 Mars 1994." *Monde Arabe: Maghred Machrek* 145 (July–September): 49–72.

Department of State. United States. 2000. "1999 Country Report on Economic Policy and Trade Practices: Tunisia." Released by the Bureau of Economic and Business Affairs, Department of State.

Deutsch, Karl. 1961. "Social Mobilization and Political Development." *American Political Science Review* 55, no. 3 (September): 493–514.

Diamond, Larry. 1992. "Economic Development and Democracy Reconsidered." *American Behavioral Scientist* 35, nos. 4–5 (March–June): 450–99. Also in *Reexamining Democracy: Essays in Honor of Seymour Martin Lipset,* ed. Gary Marks and Larry Diamond. Newbury Park, Calif.: Sage, 1992.

———. 1999. *Developing Democracy: Toward Consolidation.* Baltimore: Johns Hopkins University Press.

Diamond, Larry, Juan Linz, and Seymour Martin Lipset, eds. 1988. *Democracy in Developing Countries.* Vol. 4, *Latin America.* Boulder, Colo.: Lynne Rienner.

Duvignaud, Jean. 1970. *Change at Shebika: Report from a North African Village.* Trans. by Frances Frenaye. New York: Pantheon.

EIU (Economic Intelligence Unit). 1999. *Tunisia: Country Profile.* London: Business International.

———. 2000. *Ivory Coast: Country Profile.* London: Business International.

El-Ghonemy, M. Riad. 1990. "Land Tenure Systems and Rural Poverty in the Near East and North Africa." Study prepared for the International Fund for Agricultural Development.

———. 1996. "Recent Changes in Agrarian Reform and Rural Development Strategies in the Near East." Paper prepared for the Rural Development Agricultural Workshop, held by the Rural Development Division of the FAO in Godollo, Hungary, April 9–13.

———. 1999. "The Political Economy of Market-Based Land Reform." Popular Coalition/UNRISD monograph, June 4.

Elster, John, ed. 1986. *Rational Choice.* New York: New York University Press.

Encarnacion, Omar. 1996. "The Politics of Dual Transitions." *Comparative Politics* 28, no. 4 (July): 477–92.

———. 2000. "Beyond Transitions: The Politics of Democratic Consolidation." *Comparative Politics* 32, no. 4 (July): 479–98.

Ensminger, Jean. 1992. *Making a Market: The Institutional Transformation of an African Society.* Cambridge: Cambridge University Press.

Entelis, John, and Gregory White. 1995. "The Republic of Tunisia." In *The Government and Politics of the Middle East and North Africa,* ed. David E. Long and Bernard Reich. 3rd ed. Boulder, Colo.: Westview.

Fandy, Mamoun. 1994. "Egypt's Islamic Group: Regional Revenge?" *Middle East Journal* 48, no. 4 (autumn): 607–25.

———. 1999. "Tunisia's Emerging Democracy." *Christian Science Monitor,* October 27, p. 8.

FAO (Food and Agriculture Organization). United Nations. 1993. *Study of Land Transactions in Tunisia.*

———. 1994. *Étude Multidimensionnelle et Comparative des Régimes de Tenures Foncieres Communales et Privées en Afrique: Le Cas de Tunisie.*

Ferchiou, Sophia. 1991. *Hasab wa Nasab: Parenté, Alliance, et Patrimoine en Tunisie.* Paris: Éditions du Centre National de la Recherche Scientifique.

Foweraker, J. 1994. "Popular Political Organization and Democratization: A Comparison of Spain and Mexico." In *Developing Democracy: Comparative Research in Honour of J. F. P. Blondel,* ed. Ian Budge and David H. McKay. London: Sage.

Fraenkel, Richard, and Mathew Shane. 1974. "Land Transfer and Technical Change in a Dualistic Agriculture: A Case Study from Northern Tunisia." Staff paper 74-24. St. Paul: Department of Agriculture and Applied Economics, University of Minnesota.

Freedom House. 1999. *Freedom in the World, 1998–1999: Tunisia.* Also at <http://freedomhouse.org/survey99/country/tunisia.html>, accessed August 6, 2002.

"Freethought Traditions in the Arab World." 1995. *Freethought History Newsletter* 13. Also at <http://www.sdsmt.edu/student-orgs/tfs/reading/freethought/islam.html>, accessed August 5, 2002.

Gendzier, Irene. 1985. *Managing Political Change: Social Scientists and the Third World.* Boulder, Colo.: Westview.

Gharbi, Mohamed. 1998. "Terres Privées, Collectives, et Domaniales en Tunisie." In *Land Reform, Land Settlement, and Cooperatives 1998/1,* FAO. Also at <ftp://ftp.fao.org/sd/sda/sdaa/LR98_1/art6.pdf>, accessed August 6, 2002.

Gil, F. Acolti. 1972. "Recent Evolution of Ownership and Land Tenure in Tunisia." Instituto di Economia e Politica Agraria, Centro di Geographia Agraria. University of Padua, miscellaneous papers 1.

Gore, Charles. 2000. "The Rise and Fall of the Washington Consensus as a Paradigm for Developing Countries." *World Development* 28, no. 5: 789–804.

Gramsci, Antoni. 1971. *Selections from Prison Notebooks.* Edited and translated by Quintin Hoare and Geoffrey Nowell-Smith. London: Lawrence and Wishart.

Grissa, Abdessaatar. 1973. *Agricultural Policies and Employment: Case of Tunisia.* Paris: Organization for Economic Cooperation and Development.

Gunther, Richard, Nikiforos P. Diamandouros, and Hans-Jürgen Puhle, eds. 1995. *The Politics of Democratic Consolidation: Southern Europe in Comparative Perspective.* Baltimore: Johns Hopkins University Press.

Haggard, Stephan, and Robert Kaufman. 1992a. "Economic Adjustment and the Prospects for Democracy." In *The Politics of Economic Adjustment,* ed. Stephan Haggard and Robert Kaufman. Princeton, N.J.: Princeton University Press.

———. 1995. *The Political Economy of Democratic Transitions.* Princeton, N.J.: Princeton University Press.

———, eds. 1992b. *The Politics of Economic Adjustment.* Princeton, N.J.: Princeton University Press.

Haggard, Stephan, Jean Dominique Lafay, and Christian Morrison. 1992. "The Political Feasibility of Adjustment in Developing Countries." In *The Politics of Economic Adjustment,* ed. Stephan Haggard and Robert Kaufman. Princeton, N.J.: Princeton University Press.

Haggard, Stephan, and Steven B. Webb, eds. 1994. *Voting for Reform: Democracy, Political*

Liberalization, and Economic Adjustment. New York: Published for the World Bank by Oxford University Press.

Halliday, Fred. 1995. "The Politics of "Islam": A Second Look." *British Journal of Political Science* 25, no. 3 (July): 399–417.

Hamdi, Mohamed Elhachmi. 1998. *The Politicisation of Islam: A Case Study of Tunisia.* Boulder, Colo.: Westview.

Harber, Charles. 1973. "Tunisian Land Tenure in the Early French Protectorate." *Muslim World* 63: 307–15.

Harik, Iliya. 1984. "Continuity and Change in Local Development Policies in Egypt: From Nasser to Sadat." *International Journal of Middle East Studies* 16, no 1: 43–66.

———. 1992. "Privatization: The Issue, the Prospects, and the Fears." In *Privatization and Liberalization in the Middle East*, ed. Iliya Harik and Denis Sullivan. Bloomington: Indiana University Press.

Hayami, Yujiro, and Masao Kikuchi. 1981. *Asian Village Economy at the Crossroads: An Economic Approach to Institutional Change.* Tokyo: University of Tokyo Press; Baltimore: Johns Hopkins University Press.

———. 2001. "The Two Paths of Agrarian System Evolution in the Philippine Rice Bowl." In *Communities and Markets in Economic Development*, ed. Masahiko Aoki and Yujiro Hayami. New York: Oxford University Press.

Hedican, Edward J. "Some Issues in the Anthropology of Transaction and Exchange." *Canadian Review of Anthropology* 23, no. 1: 97–112.

Herbst, Jeffrey. 1993. *The Politics of Reform in Ghana.* Berkeley and Los Angeles: University of California Press.

Hermassi, Abdelbaki. 1972. *Leadership and National Development in North Africa.* Berkeley and Los Angeles: University of California Press.

———. 1994. "The Political and the Religious in the Modern History of the Maghreb." In *Islamism and Secularism in North Africa*, ed. John Ruedy. New York: St. Martin's Press.

Hermassi, El-Baki. 1991. "The Islamicist Movement and November 7." In *Tunisia: The Political Economy of Reform*, ed. I. William Zartman. Boulder, Colo.: Lynne Rienner.

Hinnebusch, Raymond. 1993. "Class, State, and the Reversal of Egypt's Agrarian Reform." *Middle East Report* 184 (September–October).

Hopkins, Nicholas. 1983. *Testour ou la Transformation des Compagnes Maghrebines.* Tunis: Ceres Productions.

Hopkins, Nicholas S., and Kirsten Westergaard, eds. 1998. *Directions of Change in Rural Egypt.* Cairo: The American University in Cairo Press.

Huber, Evelyn, Dietrich Rueschemeyer, and John D. Stephens. 1993. "The Impact of Economic Development on Democracy." *Journal of Economic Perspectives* 7, no. 3 (summer): 71–85.

Huntington, Samuel. 1991. *The Third Wave: Democratization in the Late Twentieth Century.* Norman: University of Oklahoma Press.

———. 1996. "Democracy for the Long Haul." *Journal of Democracy* 7, no. 2 (April): 3–13.

Huntington, Samuel, and Clement H. Moore, eds. 1970. *Authoritarian Politics in Modern Society.* New York: Basic.

Huxley, Frederick. 1990. "Development in Hammam Sousse, Tunisia: Change, Continuity, and Challenge." In *Anthropology and Development in North Africa and the Middle East*, ed. Muneera Salem-Murdock and Michael M. Horowitz, with Monica Sella. Boulder, Colo.: Westview.

Hyden, Goran. 1990. "Governance." Unpublished paper, University of Florida.

IMF (International Monetary Fund). 2001. *International Financial Statistics*. CD-ROM.

Ireton, François. 1998. "Beating Plowshares into Swords: The Relocation of Rural Egyptian Workers and Their Discontent." In *Directions of Change in Rural Egypt*, ed. Nicholas S. Hopkins and Kirsten Westergaard. Cairo: The American University of Cairo Press.

Jensen, M. C., and W. H. Meckling. 1976. "Theory of the Firm: Managerial Behavior, Agency Costs, and Ownership Structure." *Journal of Financial Economics* 3, no. 4 (October): 305–60.

Jodha, N. S. 1984. "Development Strategy for Rainfed Agriculture Possibilities and Constraints." Paper presented at a national seminar at the Institute of Economic Growth, New Delhi, India, April, 27–30.

Karl, Terry Lynn. 1990. "Dilemmas of Democratization in Latin America." *Comparative Politics* 23 (October): 1–23.

Kassab, Ahmed. 1977. "L'Emploi Rural dans les Régions de la Moyenne Medjerda." *Revue Tunisienne des Sciences Sociales* 50–51: 35–67.

Kaufman, Robert, Carlos Bazdresch, and Blanca Heredia. 1994. "Mexico: Radical Reform in a Dominant Party System." In *Voting for Reform: Democracy, Political Liberalization, and Economic Adjustment*, ed. Stephan Haggard and Steven B. Webb. New York: Published for the World Bank by Oxford University Press.

Kay, Cristobal. 1999. "Rural Development: From Agrarian Reform to Neoliberalism and Beyond." In *Latin America Transformed: Globalization and Modernity*, ed. Robert N. Gwynne and Cristobal Kay. London: Arnold; New York: Oxford University Press.

Keddie, Nikki. 1986. "The Islamist Movement in Tunisia." *Maghreb Review* 11, no. 1 (January–February): 26–39.

Kigula, J. 1993. "Land Disputes in Uganda: An Overview of the Types of Land Disputes and the Dispute Settlement Fora." Mimeograph, Makerere Institute of Social Research, Kampala.

King, Stephen. 1997. "The Politics of Market Reforms in Rural Tunisia." Ph.D. diss., Princeton University.

———. 1998. "Economic Reform and Tunisia's Hegemonic Party: The End of the Administrative Elite." *Arab Studies Quarterly* 20, no. 2 (spring): 59–86.

Kurtz, Marcus. 1995. "Urban Participation and Rural Exclusion: Neoliberal Transformation and Democratic Transition in Chile." Paper delivered to the American Political Science Association.

———. 1996. "Peasants, the State, and Democracy: Neo-liberalism and Democratic Stability in Chile, 1973–1993." Ph.D. diss., University of California, Berkeley.

Labidi, Kamel. 1999. "Real Democracy in Tunisia." *Christian Science Monitor*, November 15.

Lanjouw, Jean O. 1995. "Equilibrium Model of Land Leasing in India." Economic

Growth Center Discussion Paper no. 727 (June), Yale University. Later published as "Information and the Operation of Markets: Tests Based on a General Equilibrium Model of Land Leasing in India," *Journal of Development Economics* 60, no. 2 (December 1999): 497–527.

Lasswell, Harold Dwight. 1936. *Politics: Who Gets What, When, How.* New York: McGraw-Hill.

Lerner, Daniel. 1958. *The Passing of Traditional Society.* Glencoe, Calif.: Free Press.

Lewis, Bernard. 1988. *The Political Language of Islam.* Chicago: University of Chicago Press.

Liner, Sture. 1970. *Background Notes on Some Developments in Tunisia, September 1969– February 1970.* Tunis: United Nations Development Program.

Ling, Dwight L. 1967. *Tunisia: From Protectorate to Republic.* Bloomington: Indiana University Press.

Linz, Juan, and Alfred Stepan, eds. 1978. *The Breakdown of Democratic Regimes.* Baltimore: Johns Hopkins University Press.

Lipset, Martin. 1959. "Some Social Requisites of Democracy: Economic Development and Political Legitimacy." *American Political Science Review* 53, no. 1 (March): 69–105.

Lipton, Michael. 1977. *Why Poor People Stay Poor: Urban Bias in World Development.* Cambridge, Mass.: Harvard University Press.

Lopez, Juan. 1996. "Tunisia: Value-Added Factor Cost." Unpublished table, World Bank.

Lustig, Nora, ed. 1995. *Coping with Austerity: Poverty and Inequality in Latin America.* Washington, D.C.: The Brookings Institution.

Mackinnon, John, and Ritva Reinikka. 2000. "Lessons from Uganda on Strategies to Fight Poverty." World Bank paper. A version is at <http://econ.worldbank.org/ docs/1195.pdf>, accessed June 24, 2002.

Maghraoui, Abdeslam. 2001. "Political Authority in Crisis: Mohammed VI's Morocco." *Middle East Report* 218 (spring). Also at <http://www.merip.org/mer/mer218/218_ maghraoui.html>, accessed August 6, 2002.

Mahjoub, Azzam. 1987. "Économie et Société: La Formation du Sous-développment. L'Évolution Socio-économique de la Tunisie Précoloniale et Coloniale." In *Tunisie au Présent: Une Modernité au-dessus de Tout Soupçon?,* ed. Michel Camau, Jellal Abdelkefi, et al. Paris: Centre National de la Recherche Scientifique.

Mainwaring, Scott, and Timothy Scully, eds. 1995. *Building Democratic Institutions: Party Systems in Latin America.* Stanford, Calif.: Stanford University Press.

Makhlouf, Ezzidine. 1971. "Les Coopératives Agricoles en Tunisie: Structures et Difficultés." *Revue Tunisienne des Sciences Sociales,* no. 26: 79–114.

Mansbridge, Jane, ed. 1990. *Beyond Self-Interest.* Chicago: University of Chicago Press.

March, James, and Johan Olsen. 1984. "The New Institutionalism: Organizational Factors in Political Life." *American Political Science Review* 78, no. 3 (September): 734–49.

Markoff, John. 1996. *Waves of Democracy: Social Movements and Political Change.* Thousand Oaks, Calif.: Pine Forge.

Marks, Gary, and Larry Diamond, eds. 1992. *Reexamining Democracy: Essays in Honor of Seymour Martin Lipset.* Newbury Park, Calif.: Sage.

Marthelot, P. 1955. "Juxtaposition d'une Économie Traditionnelle et d'une Économie Moderne." *Revue de l'Institut des Belles Lettres Arabes (IBLA)* 18, no. 71: 481–501.

Maunier, R. 1927. "Recherche sur les Échanges Rituels en Afrique du Nord." *L'Année Sociologique* n.s. 2: 12–97.

Midgal, Joel. 1974. *Peasants, Politics, and Revolution: Pressures toward Political and Social Change in the Third World.* Princeton, N.J.: Princeton University Press.

Ministry of Agriculture, Tunisia. 1986. *Budget Économique..*

Mitchell, Timothy. 1999. "Dreamland: The Neoliberalism of Your Desires." *Middle East Report* 210 (spring): 28–33. Also at <http://www.merip.org/mer/mer210/210_ mitchell.html>, accessed August 6, 2002.

Montagne, Robert. 1931. *The Berbers: Their Social and Political Organization.* London: Frank Cass.

Montmartin, A., and G. Bernis. 1955. "Industrialisation et Plein Emploi en Tunisie." *Revue de l'Institut des Belles Lettres Arabes (IBLA)* 18, no. 71: 395–436.

Moore, Barrington. 1966. *Social Origins of Dictatorship and Democracy: Lord and Peasant in the Making of the Modern World.* Boston: Beacon.

Moore, Clement. 1965. *Tunisia since Independence: The Dynamics of One-Party Government.* Berkeley and Los Angeles: University of California Press.

Murphy, Emma. 1999. *Economic and Political Change in Tunisia.* New York: St. Martin's Press.

Nelson, Joan. 1992. "Poverty, Equity, and the Politics of Adjustment." In *The Politics of Economic Adjustment,* ed. Stephan Haggard and Robert R. Kaufman. Princeton, N.J.: Princeton University Press.

———, ed. 1989. *Fragile Coalitions: The Politics of Economic Adjustment.* Washington, D.C.: Overseas Development Council.

———. 1990. *Economic Crisis and Policy Choice: The Politics of Adjustment in the Third World.* Princeton, N.J.: Princeton University Press.

——— et al. 1994. *Intricate Links: Democratization and Market Reforms in Latin America and Eastern Europe.* New Brunswick, N.J.: Transaction.

North, Douglas. 1990. *Institutions, Institutional Change, and Economic Performance.* New York: Cambridge University Press.

"Nouveau Régime Foncier en Tunisie." 1959. *La Documentation Tunisienne,* series A, no. 2 (June 15).

O'Brien, Philip, and Paul Cammack, eds. 1985. *Generals in Retreat.* Manchester: Manchester University Press.

O'Donnell, Guillermo. 1973. *Modernization and Bureaucratic-Authoritarianism: Studies in South American Politics.* Berkeley: Institute of International Studies, University of California.

———. 1994. "Delegative Democracy." *Journal of Democracy* 5, no. 1 (January): 55–70. A version of this paper was presented at the Helen Kellogg Institute for International Studies and is available at <http://www.nd.edu/~kellogg/WPS/172.pdf>, accessed August 5, 2002.

———. 1996a. "Do Economists Know Best?" In *The Global Resurgence of Democracy,* ed. Larry Diamond and Mark F. Plattner. 2nd ed. Baltimore: Johns Hopkins University Press.

———. 1996b. "Illusions about Consolidation." *Journal of Democracy* 7, no. 2 (April): 34–51.

O'Donnell, Guillermo, and Philippe C. Schmitter. 1986. *Transitions from Authoritarian*

Rule: Tentative Conclusions about Uncertain Democracies. Baltimore: Johns Hopkins University Press.

Olcott, Martha Brill, and Marina Ottaway. 1999. "The Challenges of Semi-Authoritarianism." Paper from the Carnegie Endowment for International Peace. A version is at <http://www.ceip.org/programs/democr/Semi-Authoritarianism%20WP.htm>, accessed June 24, 2002.

Olsen, Mancur. 1971. *The Logic of Collective Action.* Cambridge, Mass.: Harvard University Press.

Payne, Rhys. 1991. "Economic Crisis and Policy Reform in the 1980s." In *Polity and Society in Contemporary North Africa,* ed. I. William Zartman and William Mark Habeeb. Boulder, Colo.: Westview.

Peysonnel, J. A. 1838. *Voyage dans les Régences de Tunis et d'Alger.* Paris: Poiret.

Pfiefer, Karen. 1999. "How Tunisia, Morocco, Jordan, and Even Egypt Became IMF 'Success Stories' in the 1990s." *Middle East Report* no. 210 (spring): 23–27.

Plevin, Richard. 1999. "The World Bank Project Subverts Land Reform in Brazil." *Global Exchange,* August 6. At <http://www.mstbrazil.org/wbsubverts.html>, accessed June 24, 2002.

Polanyi, Karl. 1957. *The Great Transformation.* Boston: Beacon.

Poncet, Jean. 1962. *La Colonisation et l'Agriculture Européenes en Tunisie.* Paris: Mouton.

Popkin, Samuel. 1979. *The Rational Peasant.* Berkeley and Los Angeles: University of California Press.

Przeworski, Adam, and Henry Teune. 1970. *The Logic of Comparative Inquiry.* New York: John Wiley and Sons.

Przeworski, Adam, et al. 1995. *Sustainable Democracy.* Cambridge: Cambridge University Press.

Putnam, Robert. 1995. "Bowling Along: America's Declining Social Capital." *Journal of Democracy* 6, no. 1 (January): 65–78.

Radwan, Samir Muhammad, Vali Jamal, and Ajit Kumar Ghose. 1991. *Tunisia: Rural Labour and Structural Transformation.* London: Routledge.

Richards, Alan, and John Waterbury. 1996. *A Political Economy of the Middle East.* 2nd ed. Boulder, Colo.: Westview.

Roberts, Richard. 1976. "The Failure of Agrarian Reform in Tunisia: An Alternative Hypothesis." Paper presented as part of an MA thesis, Simon Fraser University, British Columbia.

Rodrik, Dani. 1992. "The Rush to Free Trade in the Developing World: Why So Late? Why Now? Will It Last?" National Bureau of Economic Research, working paper no. 3947. Also published in *Voting for Reform: Democracy, Political Liberalization, and Economic Adjustment,* ed. Stephan Haggard and Steven B. Webb (New York: Published for the World Bank by Oxford University Press, 1994).

———. 1996. "Understanding Economic Policy Reform." *Journal of Economic Literature* 24: 9–41.

Rogowski, Ronald. 1989. *Commerce and Coalitions: How Trade Affects Domestic Political Alignments.* Princeton, N.J.: Princeton University Press.

RSF (Reporters sans Frontières). 1999. "Silence, On Réprime." Rapports Moyen-Orient. Also at <http://www.rsf.org/article.php3?id_article=925>, accessed August 5, 2002.

Rudolph, Lloyd I., and Susanne Rudolph. 1987. *In Pursuit of Lakshmi: The Political Economy of the Indian State*. Chicago: University of Chicago Press.

Rueschemeyer, Dietrich, Evelyn Stephens, and John Stephens. 1992. *Capitalist Development and Democracy*. Chicago: University of Chicago Press.

Rustow, Dankwart A. 1970. "Transitions to Democracy: Toward a Dynamic Model." *Comparative Politics* 2, no. 3 (April): 337–63.

Saad, Reem. 1999. "State, Landlord, Parliament, and Peasant: The Story of the 1992 Land Tenancy Law in Egypt." In *Agriculture in Egypt: From Pharaonic to Modern Times*, ed. Alan Bowman and Eugene Rogan. Oxford: Oxford University Press.

Sadowski, Yahya M. 1991. *Political Vegetables: Businessman and Bureaucrat in the Development of Egyptian Agriculture*. Washington, D.C.: The Brookings Institution.

Schamis, Hector. 1991. "Reconceptualizing Latin American Authoritarianism in the 1970s: From Bureaucratic Authoritarianism to Neoconservatism." *Comparative Politics* 23, no. 2 (January): 201–20.

———. 1999. "Distributional Coalitions and the Politics of Economic Reform in Latin America." *World Politics* 2, no. 51 (January): 236–68.

Schmitter, Philippe C. 1974. "Still the Century of Corporatism?" *The Review of Politics* 36: 85–131. Reprinted in *Trends towards Corporatist Intermediation*, ed. Philippe C. Schmitter and Gerhard Lehmbruch. London and Beverly Hills: Sage, 1979.

———. 1992. "Interest Systems and the Consolidation of Democracies." In *Reexamining Democracy: Essays in Honor of Seymour Martin Lipset*, ed. Gary Marks and Larry Diamond. Newbury Park, Calif.: Sage.

———. 1995. "Organized Interests and Democratic Consolidation in Southern Europe." In *The Politics of Democratic Consolidation: Southern Europe in Comparative Perspective*, ed. Richard Gunther, Nikiforos P. Diamandouros, and Hans-Jürgen Puhle. Baltimore. Johns Hopkins University Press.

Scott, Christopher. 1996. "The Distributive Impact of the New Economic Model in Chile." In *The New Economic Model in Latin America and Its Impact on Income Distribution and Poverty*, ed. Victor Bulmer-Thomas. New York: St. Martin's Press.

Scott, James. 1976. *The Moral Economy of the Peasant*. New Haven, Conn.: Yale University Press.

———. 1985. *Weapons of the Weak: Everyday Forms of Peasant Resistance*. New Haven, Conn.: Yale University Press.

Sebag, Paul. 1951. *La Tunisie: Essai de Monographie*. Paris: Éditions Sociales.

Sen, Amartya. 1990. "Rational Fools." In *Beyond Self-Interest*, ed. Jane Mansbridge. Chicago: University of Chicago Press.

Simmons, John. 1970. "Land Reform in Tunisia." USAID country paper.

———, ed. 1974. *Village and Family: Essays on Rural Tunisia*. HRAFLEx Books, Ethnography Series. New Haven, Conn.: Human Relations Area Files.

Skocpol, Theda. 1979. *States and Social Revolutions: A Comparative Analysis of France, Russia, and China*. Cambridge: Cambridge University Press.

Slama, Bice. 1970. *L'Insurrection de 1864 en Tunisie*. Tunis: Maison Tunisienne de l'Édition.

Solimano, Andres. 1999. "Beyond Unequal Development: An Overview." World Bank paper, March. Also at <http://www.worldbank.org/html/dec/Publications/Workpapers/wps2000series/wps2091/wps2091.pdf>, accessed June 24, 2002.

Springborg, Robert. 1990. "Agrarian Bourgeoisie, Semiproletarians, and the Egyptian State: Lessons for Liberalization." *International Journal of Middle East Studies* 22, no. 4: 447–72.

———. 1991. "State-Society Relations in Egypt: The Debate over Owner-Tenant Relations." *Middle East Journal* 45, no. 2 (spring): 232–49.

Stallings, Barbara. 1990. "Politics and Economic Crisis: A Comparative Study of Chile, Peru, and Columbia." In *Economic Crisis and Policy Change: The Politics of Adjustment in the Third World,* ed. Joan Nelson. Princeton, N.J.: Princeton University Press.

Swidler, Anne. 1986. "Culture in Action: Symbols and Strategies." *American Sociological Review* 51 (April): 273–86.

Tarrow, Sidney. 1995. "Mass Mobilization and Regime Change." In *The Politics of Democratic Consolidation: Southern Europe in Comparative Perspective,* ed. Richard Gunther, Nikiforos P. Diamandouros, and Hans-Jürgen Puhle. Baltimore: Johns Hopkins University Press.

Taylor, Lance. 1991. *Income Distribution, Inflation, and Growth.* Cambridge, Mass.: MIT Press.

———, ed. 1999. *After Neoliberalism: What Next for Latin America?* Ann Arbor: University of Michigan Press.

Taylor, Michael. 1982. *Community, Anarchy, and Liberty.* Cambridge: Cambridge University Press.

Tessler, Mark, Gregory White, and John Entelis. 1989. "Some Lessons from the Study of Political and Social Attitude Changes in Tunisia." Paper presented at the Tunisia Country Day Program of SAIS, Washington, D.C.

———. 1995. "The Republic of Tunisia." In *The Government and Politics of the Middle East and North Africa,* ed. David E. Long and Bernard Reich. 3rd ed. Boulder, Colo.: Westview.

Thorner, David, Basile H. Kerblay, and R. E. F. Smith. 1986. *A. V. Chayanov on the Theory of Peasant Economy.* Madison: University of Wisconsin Press.

Uphoff, Norman. 1992. *Learning from Gal Oya: Possibilities for Participatory Development and Post-Newtonian Social Science.* Ithaca, N.Y.: Cornell University Press.

Uphoff, Norman, and Milton Esman. 1974. *Local Organization for Rural Development: Analysis of Asian Experience.* Ithaca, N.Y.: Rural Development Committee, Cornell University.

Valensi, Lucette. 1977. *L'Économie Rurale et la Vie des Campagnes au 18e et 19e Siécles.* Paris: Mouton.

———. 1985. *Tunisian Peasants in the Eighteenth and Nineteenth Centuries.* Cambridge: Cambridge University Press.

Van Dooren, P. J. 1968. "State-Controlled Changes in Tunisia's Agrarian Structure." *Tropical Man* 1: 59–108.

Vandewalle, Dirk J. 1989. *Ben Ali's New Tunisia.* Field staff reports no. 8. Indianapolis: Universities Field Staff International.

———, ed. 1996. *North Africa: Development and Reform in a Changing Global Economy.* New York: St. Martin's Press.

Wade, Robert. 1988. *Village Republics.* Cambridge: Cambridge University Press.

Waisman, Carlos. 1992. "Capitalism, the Market, and Democracy." *American Behavioral Scientist* 35, nos. 4–5 (March–June): 500–16.

Waltz, Susan. 1989. "Particularism and Reform in Ben Ali's Tunisia." Paper presented at the SAIS Tunisia Conference Day, Washington, D.C., April 4–5.

Ware, L. B. 1988. "Ben Ali's Constitutional Coup in Tunisia." *Middle East Journal* 42, no. 4 (autumn): 587–601.

Waterbury, John. 1970. *The Commander of the Faithful.* New York: Columbia University Press.

———. 1989. "The Political Management of Economic Adjustment and Economic Reform." In *Fragile Coalitions: The Politics of Economic Adjustment,* ed. Joan Nelson. Washington, D.C.: Overseas Development Council.

———. 1991. "Peasants Defy Categorization." In *Peasants and Politics in the Modern Middle East,* ed. Farhad Kazemi and John Waterbury. Miami: Florida International University Press.

———. 1993. *Exposed to Innumerable Delusions: Public Enterprise and State Power in Egypt, India, Mexico, and Turkey.* Ithaca, N.Y.: Cornell University Press.

Whitehead, Laurence. 1986. "International Aspects of Democratization." In *Transitions from Authoritarian Rule: Comparative Perspectives,* ed. Guillermo O'Donnell, Philippe C. Schmitter, and Laurence Whitehead. Baltimore: Johns Hopkins University Press.

Wildawsky, Aaron. 1987. "Choosing Preferences by Constructing Institutions: A Cultural Theory of Preference Formation." *American Political Science Review* 81, no. 1: 3–21.

Williamson, John. 1990. "What Washington Means by Policy Reform." In *Latin American Adjustment: How Much Has Happened?* ed. John Williamson. Washington, D.C.: Institute for International Economics.

———. 1993. "Democracy and the Washington Consensus." *World Development* 21, no. 8: 1329–36.

Wolf, Eric R. 1969. *Peasant Wars of the Twentieth Century.* New York: Harper and Row.

World Bank. 1975. *The Assault on World Poverty: Problems of Rural Development, Education, and Health.* Baltimore: Published for the World Bank by Johns Hopkins University Press.

———. 1986a. *Report and Recommendation of the President of the International Bank for Reconstruction and Development to the Executive Directors on a Proposed Loan in an Amount Equivalent to U.S. $150.0 Million to the Republic of Tunisia for an Agricultural Sector Adjustment Loan.* Washington, D.C.: World Bank.

———. 1986b. *Republic of Tunisia, Agricultural Sector Adjustment Loan: Medium-Term Agricultural Sector Adjustment Program.* Washington, D.C.: World Bank.

———. 1990. *World Development Report 1990: Poverty.* Oxford: Oxford University Press and the World Bank.

———. 1991a. *Project Completion Report: Tunisia: Agricultural Sector Adjustment Loan 2754-Tun.*

———. 1991b. *République de Tunisie: Les Petits Agriculteurs: Potentialités et Perspectives.* Étude Technique.

———. 1993. *The East Asian Miracle.* Oxford: Oxford University Press.

——. 1994. *World Development Report 1994: Infrastructure for Development*. New York: Oxford University Press and the World Bank.

——. 1995a. *Republic of Tunisia: Growth Policies and Poverty Alleviation*. 2 vols. Washington, D.C.: World Bank.

——. 1995b. *Republic of Tunisia Poverty Alleviation: Preserving Progress While Preparing for the Future*. Washington, D.C.: World Bank.

——. 1996. *Tunisia's Global Integration and Sustainable Development*. World Bank Middle East and North Africa Economic Studies. Washington, D.C.: World Bank.

——. 2000a. Draft of *World Development Report 2000/2001*.

——. 2000b. *World Development Report 2000/2001: Attacking Poverty*. Oxford: Oxford University Press. Also available at <http://www.worldbank.org/poverty/wdrpoverty/report/index.htm>, accessed August 6, 2002.

——. 2001a. *The Theory behind Market-Assisted Land Reform*. At <http://wbln0018.worldbank.org/Networks/ESSD/icdb.nsf/D4856F112E805DF4852566C9007C27A6/5B758F21508127B585256778004D0405>, accessed August 5, 2002.

——. 2001b. *World Bank Annual Report*. Vol. 1, *Year in Review*. Washington, D.C.: World Bank.

Zahra, Nadia Abu. 1982. *Sidi Ameur: A Tunisian Village*. London: Published for the Middle East Centre, St. Antony's College, Oxford, by Ithaca.

Zakaria, Fareed. 1997. "The Rise of Illiberal Democracy." *Foreign Affairs* 76, no. 6 (November–December): 22–43.

Zamiti, Khalil. 1970. "Les Obstacles Matériels et Idéologiques a l'Évolution Sociale des Compagnies Tunisiennes." *Revue Tunisienne des Sciences Sociales* 21: 9–57.

Zartman, I. William, ed. 1991. *Tunisia: The Political Economy of Reform*. Boulder, Colo.: Lynne Rienner.

Zghal, Abdelkader. 1967a. *Modernisation de l'Agriculture et Populations Semi-nomades*. The Hague: Mouton.

——. 1967b. "Systeme de Parenté et Systeme Coopératif." *Revue Tunisienne des Sciences Sociales* 11: 11–23.

——. 1973. "Peasant and Political Power in North Africa." Unpublished conference paper.

——. 1980. "L'Économie Paysanne de la Tunisie Pré-coloniale." *Revue Tunisienne de Sciences Sociales*, no. 17: 11–30.

Ziadeh, Nicola A. 1969. *Origins of Nationalism in Tunisia*. Beirut: Librarie du Liban.

Zussman, Mira. 1992. *Development and Disenchantment in Rural Tunisia: The Bourguiba Years*. Boulder, Colo.: Westview.

INDEX

Page numbers in italics refer to illustrations.

Stephen J. King
is Assistant Professor of Government
at Georgetown University.